THE FORENSIC CONSULTANT

Follow The Money, Fulfil Your Dreams…

A Forensic Mindset for Professional
Health, Wealth and Happiness…

MARTIN DOUGALL

Ultimate World Publishing
Diamond Creek,
Victoria Australia 3089
www.writeabook.com.au

DISCLAIMER

This book is based on the author's professional experiences in the field of forensic accounting and financial investigations. While the stories and insights are drawn from real-life cases, the confidentiality of clients, individuals, and organisations has been maintained in relation to information not in the public domain. To protect privacy and comply with legal and professional obligations, certain names, identifying details, and case specifics have been amended, anonymised, or adjusted where appropriate to illustrate broader themes and lessons. The content is intended for informational and educational purposes only, and any resemblance to actual persons, living or deceased, or real events is purely coincidental unless specifically stated.

DEDICATION

This book is dedicated to:

My family - to Sally, Cameron and Heather, to my Dad, Mum (gone but never forgotten), Lynn, Gary, and the boys, and to all my extended family in Scotland and beyond.

My friends - home and away, from Hamilton, Glasgow, Edinburgh, Manchester, London, Sydney, Melbourne, and Mount Eliza, and to those who have flown, far and wide, around the world.

My colleagues, past, present and future - too many to name and, but for confidentiality reasons, I would have done so in the pages of this book, I've learned so much from you.

Forensic consultants everywhere - to the seekers of truth in tangled ledgers, to the calm amidst the corporate storm, to the minds that never stop asking "why?" This book is for those who seek clarity in complexity, who see patterns in chaos, and who know that integrity isn't just a principle - it's a practice. May your lens stay sharp, your judgment steady, and your curiosity unrelenting.

CONTENTS

FOREWORD

In a world of fake news and fraudulent claims, the voice of truth, data and evidence needs to be heard.

The Forensic Consultant is not just a book. It is a voice in the darkness, shining light on a murky world of fraud, lies and deception. It is a lens into a profession where deception is discovered, where crime meets punishment, and precision makes the difference between freedom and conviction. Intellectual rigour and ethical complexity abound, and the role of the Forensic Consultant has never been more vital.

This book invites readers behind the scenes, into the boardrooms and courtrooms, where decisions are made, dilemmas are debated, and careers rise and fall. It also reveals the key elements of the forensic mindset to help navigate a career in professional services and beyond. Whether you're a professional seeking clarity, a student exploring career paths, or simply a curious mind drawn to the drama of real-world fraud and financial crime investigations, you'll find this book insightful and provocative.

The author brings not only technical expertise but also a rare ability to cut through complexity with wit and wisdom. It is also a deeply personal story of growth and development in a journey that has taken him all over the world. Through news stories, case studies, personal insights, and practical guidance, *The Forensic Consultant* canters through the decades, demystifying a world, often sensationalised in headlines, but rarely understood in depth.

As you turn these pages, be prepared to challenge assumptions, sharpen your analytical lens, and appreciate the quiet heroes who ensure that truth will prevail and the villains meet justice—with the evidence to prove it.

HEROES AND VILLAINS

In this book, I share insights from my life as an expert forensic accountant over the past three decades, and the forensic mindset I have developed, over time, to build a career that has ultimately brought me professional health, wealth and happiness. I also share stories of the heroes who inspired me, the cases I've been involved in, and the challenges and dilemmas I've faced and (mostly) overcome. Ultimately, it is about the values I hold dear, which I think have a broader resonance and can help you achieve success in whatever career you choose to pursue.

In Chapter 1, I share my story before forensic and how Billy Connolly's drive to be windswept and interesting inspired the younger me to be curious, to explore the world around me, and to bring my personality to whatever I was doing. It is vitally important to be yourself, but also be consciously aware of your personal brand, what it looks like from other perspectives, and what you want your story to be.

Chapter 2 is about being consciously aware of the importance of mindset and the values and beliefs that drive our behaviours. I had been inspired to move to London in 1997 to join the Forensic Accounting team. As I took my first steps in the world of investigations, I draw from that master fictional detective from

Baker Street, Sherlock Holmes, and his famous powers of deductive reasoning to shine a light on the dark side. I introduce the famous fraud triangle, and through the lens of real-life fraud investigations, I provide insights on motives, beliefs and values, how to build your deductive reasoning, and how awareness of the dark side can help you be consciously aware of what is important to you and how to navigate the inevitable dilemmas that come along.

In Chapter 3, having moved to Australia in 1999, I share my experience of the Sydney 2000 Olympics and how Cathy Freeman rose to the occasion to inspire me, a nation and the world. My time in Sydney took me deep into the world of litigation, valuation and billion-dollar disputes. These cases taught me to think deeply, develop and support my views, and consider arguments and counter-arguments with lawyers. There are also times in a career when we all have to rise to the occasion and win that medal. Whether it's a promotion, a presentation, or an important piece of work, having the right mindset with the discipline and dedication to do the right things consistently can be the training muscle that makes all the difference.

Chapter 4 shows my curiosity, courage and openness to new opportunities, which led me to London and Sydney, but now took me back to Scotland for both business and personal reasons. I give some insights from the story of Marie Curie, whose groundbreaking work and work ethic led to the discoveries of polonium and radium and ultimately two Nobel Prizes, which became particularly personal to me when I moved back to Edinburgh. She was driven by a desire for truth, not personal glory, and bringing people along with her, which I increasingly found essential to leading, growing and managing effective teams.

In Chapter 5, I share the story of Frank J. Wilson, widely considered to be the father of forensic accounting, for his pivotal role in investigating alleged tax evasion by Al Capone in the 1930s, which finally brought down Chicago's most notorious gangster. Whilst Kevin Costner gets the glory as Elliot Ness in the *Untouchables* movie of the 1980s, it was Wilson who led a painstaking review of Al Capone's business practices, tax and accounting records that ultimately led to his indictment and imprisonment. In multiple cases over many years, those consistent, unglamourous disciplines of perseverance, resilience and process to establish the facts, analyse the evidence, and follow the money have been essential building blocks to uncover truth and be successful over the long run. There are no shortcuts to building your reputation over a long career, but doing the right things consistently and protecting your integrity and reputation will become your most valuable asset, particularly when facing criminality.

With Chapter 6, I return to the sporting theme and the incredible story of Tom Brady, the seven-time Super Bowl winner with the New England Patriots and Tampa Bay Buccaneers, who retired at 45 after an unparalleled career. He wasn't always destined for greatness. 198 players were selected before him in the 2000 NFL draft, with only 55 chosen after him. At that time, my career prospects were similar. Good enough to play, but no one was predicting a stellar career. Whilst Tom Brady became the Greatest of All Time in his chosen sport through belief, consistency, dedication and determination, my path was more modest, but some important lessons laid the foundation for me. The most critical step was exorcising the imposter syndrome, which had acted as a handbrake on the first decade of my career.

In Chapter 7, as the world learned a new lexicon of subprime mortgages and collateralised debt obligations in the Global Financial Crisis of 2008, a much older fraud known as a Ponzi scheme made a comeback with a new villain, Bernie Madoff. This was boom-time for forensic accountants with multiple investigations as economies teetered and banker bailouts proliferated. Harry Markopolos became one such hero with his investigation into the Madoff Investment Securities Ponzi scheme, which defrauded investors of an estimated $64 billion. A meticulous, sceptical forensic mindset was essential and honing those skills in my own investigations also began to resonate in the wider leadership roles I was taking on. I knew my strengths and weaknesses, and a more forensic framework for considering which roles to take on and which to avoid began to crystallise in my mind.

In Chapter 8, it's 2010, and I'm in Manchester with one of my heroes, Sir Alex Ferguson, the legendary manager of Manchester United. In my Partner interview, my pitch was to tell the story of another Scot who came to Manchester and became massively successful. It wasn't subtle, but the combination of personality, promise and potential - make me a Partner, and I'll make you successful – created a vision of where I was from and where I was going. This ultimately led to opportunities for me to lead our Forensic and then wider Risk Consulting teams in the UK outside London. Leadership qualities, including confidence, effective communication, and cultivating a winning mindset in teams, whether in sports or business, require drive, determination, and a compelling vision for your team. A combination of consistency, confidence and a dash of creativity could set you up to do the same.

Chapter 9 shows the aftermath of the Global Financial Crisis: fraud was on the rise, and fraudsters were evolving. The award-winning movie, *Catch Me If You Can*, starring Leonardo DiCaprio as Frank Abagnale, had some interesting parallels to the typical fraudsters I was encountering. Frank was a conman specialising in impersonation, forgery, cheque fraud and innovative use of technology. He impersonated a pilot, a doctor and a lawyer, among others, before his arrest, conviction and subsequent role as expert consultant on fraud prevention. I could do the latter without ever doing the former, and it led me into some fascinating discoveries on human nature and the use of technology for good and ill.

In Chapter 10, I've taken on the biggest challenge of my career to date to lead and grow a Forensic business in Australia, and I reflect on what went well, what could have been done differently, and a wide and varied range of cases. As a leader coming to a new market, I looked to Andrew Carnegie for inspiration in building a team of many talents around me. The right people doing the right things in the right roles.

In Chapter 11, it's 2020, and the world has been shaken by the Covid pandemic. Warren Buffett was right that you only see who is swimming naked when the tide goes out. From 2020 onwards, the tide was truly out, revealing myriad examples of fraud and financial crime. I share some insights on seeing and taking advantage of opportunities, understanding the impact of incentives and narratives on human behaviour, and provide some ideas on how to build your professional brand and reputation to capitalise on the opportunities in your domain.

Finally, in Chapter 12, I bring it all together with Dale Carnegie's famous tome, *How to Win Friends and Influence People*. His guide shows how to build positive relationships by being genuinely interested in people, appreciative, empathetic, and taking the time to listen and understand other people's perspectives. These are fantastic attributes to consciously develop, no matter what business or role you are in, and the mindset of having people at the centre of what you are trying to achieve is always worth the investment. These are precious years, and it's important to spend the time doing what you enjoy and what has purpose and passion for you. I've loved the opportunity to follow the money and fulfil my dreams, and it has truly led to professional health, wealth, and happiness for me.

Whilst I've tried to pick out the James Bond moments in this book, I summarise the key steps here to foster your own forensic mindset to help advance your career and fulfil your dreams. I hope you find this interesting and I would love to hear from you if you do….

CHAPTER 1

WINDSWEPT AND INTERESTING

"Before you judge a man, walk a mile in his shoes. After that, who cares?... He's a mile away and you've got his shoes!"

Billy Connolly

Local Hero

Billy Connolly is one of my heroes.

As a young lad growing up in a small town near Glasgow, I discovered Billy's unique sense of humour, which really resonated with me, over school lunchtimes shared with a couple of classmates. Our daily ritual was a 15-minute walk from Hamilton Grammar School through the town, buying sandwiches and sweets along the way, then on to my mates' dad's car, which was parked outside his work. Access to the car was a godsend, particularly in the dreich Scottish winters, providing shelter and heat from the elements and, crucially, a cassette player to help us escape from the monotony of maths and science to stories from the Clyde shipyards, the Edinburgh Festival and London's famous Royal Albert Hall.

Billy tells the story of his first visit to the Edinburgh Festival, the world's largest arts festival, as a young man in the early 1960s. At the time, he was working as a welder in the shipyards and had gone with his mates for a pub crawl along Edinburgh's famous Rose Street. On that trip, for the first time, he came across some arty guys with long hair and earrings. People were staring at them. But as laughter turned to wonder, in that instant, Billy decided he wanted to be one of them! He started growing his hair and modelling his trademark look, and his journey to becoming *"windswept and interesting,"* the aptly named title of his best-selling autobiography, was on its way.

Years later, having followed the school-to-university-to-work regime common to many of my peers, I qualified as a chartered accountant with Coopers & Lybrand, a predecessor firm to PwC. After a few years of learning the ropes as an auditor, I attended a careers fair run by the other divisions in the firm. I learned a little of what the Tax, Transactions, Restructuring and Corporate Finance teams focused on. Then, without fanfare or expectation, a Partner in the 'Forensic' team stood up to speak: *"In Forensic, we do stuff for money. There are no fixed budgets, every case is different, and we use our intellect, experience and expertise to figure it out."*

I was intrigued and instantly hooked. Like Billy in Edinburgh, this was my lightbulb moment. I was curious. I wanted to be one of them.

A secondment to the big smoke in London followed, and my journey into the world of fraud, bribery, corruption and money laundering investigations had begun.

In the Audience

Back in 1985, in *An Audience with Billy Connolly*, he played to a packed crowd of celebrities and fans, and the result was a best-selling video of the performance. In that room were significant luminaries of the day, such as Bob Geldof, Eric Clapton, Joanna Lumley and Dennis Law.

In front of a pink neon sign of his name, Billy had the audience in tears of laughter in a spellbinding 90-minute performance. There are some wonderful sketches of observational humour, questioning the world he sees around him, and even suggesting a new upbeat national anthem to replace "God Save The Queen."

The cassette of that performance became a staple of lunchtimes for three young lads in Scotland. We loved his description of his singing voice *"like a goose farting in the fog,"* traditional Scottish entertainers as *"singing shortbread tins,"* and questioning *"who the sign to the braille school is for."* If you haven't seen it, it is well worth finding on YouTube.

Around that time, at age 13, I was making my first forays into high school. I would have loved to have been able to tell stories like Billy, but I was young, shy, quite clever, but lacking in confidence.

My first 'job' was as school bookie taking bets on such surefire things as Scotland winning the World Cup. It never happened, of course, but it gave my creativity and love of numbers an avenue to explore. The focus was on sporting events: the World Cup, the Scottish Premier League, and the Super Bowl, an exotic new craze recently imported from America. I loved setting the odds, working out the risk and reward (at a very basic level), and seeing how it all panned out.

The money was trivial, of course (pocket money was tight in those days!), and I wasn't really aware at the time, but it gave me a playground to learn about incentives, human nature, testing the boundaries and working out the odds. I enjoyed the game more than the outcome, but I knew even then that some discipline and ground rules were vital, and not being swayed by emotion was important to having a sweetie fund at the end of the day.

Visiting Algebra

One of my favourite quotes from Billy is *"I don't know why I should have to learn Algebra.... I'm never likely to go there."* Well, given my particular brain, I did have to go there, and I actually quite liked it.

At school, I had an unusual combination of capabilities, being proficient in both Maths, which I inherited from Mum, a Primary School teacher and Maths scholar in her youth, and English, which I inherited from Dad, a gregarious and expressive lecturer in English and Drama with a keen sense of humour. My favourite subject was Modern Studies, a distinct subject in the Scottish education system, focusing on contemporary political and social issues, domestic and international, aimed at developing knowledge of the modern world, its political processes and social challenges.

I also had blind spots, notably all things scientific. I remember struggling through my mandatory science subject, Physics, until a particularly insightful tutor taught me to look at it all as Applied Maths and my route through the exam (if not my in-depth understanding of the subject) was clear.

As anyone who knows me well will attest, I was and am hopeless at all things practical.

Dad would say to me, *"All your brains are in your head, son, and you'll need to earn enough money to pay all those tradesmen to do those things where you're incompetent."*

And he was right.

I would later understand that this was a division of labour and comparative advantage that Adam Smith, the father of Economics and a fellow Scot, would talk about in his seminal work, *An Enquiry into the Nature and Causes of the Wealth of Nations*.

As school progressed, my competence with numbers (and incompetence with science) led me first into Accounting and later into Economics. In my experience, very few people grow up dreaming of becoming an accountant, and I certainly didn't. However, competence and some level of achievement in a subject, particularly one with a potential career path to finance the future cost of tradesmen, became more viable in the absence of alternatives.

I flirted with the idea of sports journalism (being paid to go to big sporting events was certainly attractive, and I could write a decent article), but the path seemed narrow and hazardous. I also explored where Modern Studies could take me, but the spectrum from social work to politics to academia also fizzled out.

My residual competence with numbers meant that when it was time to apply for universities, a combination of Accounting and Economics seemed sensible. I knew my strengths (and weaknesses), and making the sensible choice to play to those strengths in how I would spend the next few years was a natural progression. That said, I was only 17 and there was plenty of time to change my mind if it all became too difficult, too dull, or too demanding.

It wasn't quite the same for Billy, who left school and became a welder: "*I was actually becoming an engineer, and I joined the wrong queue. And so, I became a welder, without knowing what a welder was.*"

It was a long way from the windswept and interesting world-famous comedian and actor he would ultimately become, but the environment, the characters, and the people he met in the shipyards became a source of inspiration and fundamental to his stories. Much of that storytelling is self-deprecating, self-aware and infused with a sense of his own limitations, and I really enjoyed it.

We had very different paths, but the people I grew up with and the characters I came across in the Scotland of the 1980s, and that self-deprecating, self-awareness and search for humour in every situation also resonated with me.

I have always been acutely aware of my limitations but also my strengths. I could focus on details, on what is important, and constantly refine and improve my craft. In much the same way, Billy's end product is inspired by his environment but honed by repetition and refinement, so the delivery is seamless and appears effortless.

That similar forensic attention to detail helped hone my exam technique at school and beyond, and also set in train my future path to becoming a forensic accountant without knowing, at that stage, what a forensic accountant actually was.

Glasgow Smiles Better

In the 1980s, a campaign was launched to promote the city of Glasgow as a tourist destination and an attractive location for industry. This was no mean feat, as Glasgow in the 1970s was known for its economic decline, high levels of poverty and inequality following de-industrialisation, and the unemployment and social problems which followed. The campaign logo was a large yellow Mr Happy smile, and it helped Glasgow turn the corner and project a more positive image to the world.

As the decade progressed, confidence improved, and important events such as the Glasgow Garden Festival of 1988 and becoming the first city in the UK to be named European Capital of Culture in 1990 had a lasting positive impact. It was this revitalised city that became central to me for the next eight years.

In 1989, I went to the University of Strathclyde to study Accounting and Economics through a process of elimination - I was no good at science, and I would need a job, so it had to be business-related.

At University, I added elective courses on US politics, law and Italian (I had been on holiday the previous summer and thought it would improve my romantic prospects to speak the language), in my own attempt to become windswept and interesting. I was involved in the Christian Union and enjoyed the freedom and rhythms of University life.

I stayed on for an Honours year and, through a couple of eclectic Accounting tutors, I survived a detour into French feminism, philosophy and communism, and a dissertation on the pros and cons of food aid to developing economies. I also needed a job, so flush with my degree, I secured a position on the graduate audit scheme at Coopers & Lybrand.

In 1993, my first day in the office involved being sent in my shiny new suit with my brand-new briefcase to audit… my old University.

I learned a lot over the next four years. University was good for theory, but working on-site at a range of clients from councils to conglomerates, whisky distilleries to wholesale grocers, and utilities to universities taught me so much more.

Auditing was practical, pragmatic, and people-oriented, requiring analytical thinking and attention to detail, which were foundational for my future career. Additionally, it required being organised, adaptable, and capable of working under pressure. The challenge was also there in the first few years, with natural progression from junior to more complex parts of the audit file and then onto being in charge on a number of audits. The environment in Glasgow was commercial and competitive, but also had a good level of camaraderie and banter.

I tried to look at my audit work from the perspective of the finance staff who prepared the material and their incentives and motivations to get through the process. I also thought about how I came across and how I wanted the next stage of my career to develop.

I had enjoyed my time as an auditor, but having qualified as a Chartered Accountant and seeing my peers start to go on international secondments, I also thought about what was next. It was with this mindset that I attended a careers fair at the end of 1996.

500 Miles

The best-known song of the Scottish band The Proclaimers is "I'm Gonna Be (500 Miles)," which also happens to be my go-to karaoke song (essentially shouting rather than singing!).

In 1997, it was time for me to branch out from Glasgow smiles to roughly 500 miles south on the M6 and M1 to London (it's actually 413 miles according to Google).

I was equipped with an upbringing, a qualification, and a few years of work experience. Equally important, I had a curiosity, inquisitiveness and desire to see the world. I may not have known it at the time, but I also had the beginnings of a forensic mindset as I embarked on my career as a forensic accountant.

CHAPTER 2

ELEMENTAL VALUES

"When you have eliminated the impossible, whatever remains, however improbable, must be the truth."

Sherlock Holmes

London Calling

In 1997, I had been inspired to move to London to join the exciting new world of Forensic Accounting and take my first tentative steps to becoming an investigator.

I had grown up devouring the novels of Sir Arthur Conan Doyle and tales of his masterful fictional detective, Sherlock Holmes.

Winding my way down to Baker Street for the first time, I could feel the weight of Victorian London from the plotlines of *The Sign of Four*, *The Valley of Fear* and even *The Hound of the Baskervilles*, which begins in London.

Baker Street, Scotland Yard, Paddington Station, the Houses of Parliament – these venues all felt familiar to me from the stories of my youth. Even the Embankment location of my first office in London carried memories of a scene from *A Study in Scarlet* where Holmes and Watson attend a concert, whilst on the trail of the mysterious murder of Enoch Drebber.

My working journey quickly moved to Plumtree Court, an old alley near Holborn, and it was here that I began one of my first cases, assessing loss and damages following a fire at the premises of a mountain bike manufacturer. There was nothing suspicious about the fire, but the task at hand was to assess the consequential loss to the company from the remaining records, which survived the fire.

Incomplete was an understatement.

In the days before widespread servers, backups and electronic records, we had to work with what we had, reconstruct where possible, make some (what we felt were) reasonable assumptions, and plot what we thought would have happened to the pedal-powered profits 'but for' the fire.

Unsurprisingly, the results had tailed off, but to what extent was this due to the fire or the myriad other possible factors, and what would have happened had the fire not occurred? A detailed forensic impact assessment followed, including a review of historical performance, reliability against budgets, and known contemporaneous plans and projections. Our picture slowly became clearer.

This case was my first introduction to lawyers, insurers and the power of competing narratives. The company was not (as it foretold) on the verge of stratospheric growth, only to be thwarted by a devastating fire. Equally, it was not (as the insurers may have preferred) on the brink of financial ruin, looking for a massive but fraudulent insurance windfall. Whilst the narratives were not so extreme, positions were adopted, and lawyers for both sides looked to their respective forensic accounting independent experts to bring their experience and expertise to bear.

Fortunately, we had such an expert.

A senior Partner on our team had worked on many such cases and was, Holmes-like, able to cut through the impossible and improbable, and based on our factual analysis, determine his opinion on what he thought the financial position would have been 'but for' the fire. The forensic accountant on the other side had done a similar analysis, and whilst his opinion arrived at a different number, the range between the parties narrowed considerably, and a sensible negotiated settlement was achieved.

I was thrilled to have been involved. I loved getting into the detailed factual analysis of what had happened and the reconstruction (to the extent possible) of the financial records of the business. I was also stimulated by the intellectual challenge of determining a 'best guess' of what would have happened but for the fire and wading through the likelihood and impact of the myriad possible factors.

This interplay of historical fact in terms of what had happened, the truth that Holmes was so good at deducing, combined with opinion based on experience and expertise, was fascinating to me. Through this and other similar cases over the coming months, my move to London was vindicated.

The Mysteries Deepen

My next case took me to the heart of the United Nations.

In the early 1990s, following the invasion and occupation of Kuwait by Iraq, and subsequent liberation by a United Nations-authorised international coalition, there were a number of claims for loss and damage suffered as a result of what became known as the Gulf War.

In response, the United Nations Compensation Commission (UNCC) was created in 1991, as a subsidiary of the United Nations Security Council, with a mandate to process claims and pay compensation for losses, including loss of property, deaths, natural resources, damage to public health and environmental damage. By the time the work of the UNCC officially came to a close in 2022, it had considered more than two million claims for compensation, totalling over US$350 billion.

By 1998, lawyers and forensic accountants were in full swing assessing the legal basis, contemporaneous evidence, and quantum of such losses in commercial cases for the UNCC. Many of these cases were considered in London, as a globally recognised centre for arbitration and commercial dispute resolution.

In one case, we were engaged to assess the loss suffered as a result of various assets, such as plant, equipment and machinery, which were destroyed during the invasion and its aftermath, as well as the consequential loss of profit, which would have been earned by joint venture partners under contracts, but which could not be fulfilled because of the war.

Again, contemporaneous records were incomplete and, in many cases, unavailable. However, an assessment had to be made based on what was available, and in accordance with the relevant legal and accounting principles in the assessment of loss and fulfilment of contracts.

Another case took me in a completely different direction as I became an expert (somewhat reluctantly, it has to be said!) on expected milk yields of cows in rural England. This case involved a mysterious and widespread outbreak of mastitis in a herd of cows, allegedly caused by environmental pathogens spread by a nearby business, which dramatically reduced the milk yield of the herd.

Fortunately, the *John Nix Farm Management Pocketbook* was to hand as the purported bible of all things agricultural, including expected litres of milk per day, peak production periods, and typical lactation curves, not to mention the varying yield expectations of the Holstein-Friesian, Guernsey, Jersey and Ayrshire varieties of cows. I also learned about other factors impacting milk production, including the specific genetics, diet and environment of each herd of cows. Everything you could ever possibly want to know!

Many weeks were spent determining and disentangling causation and consequence, actual and expected yields, and adjusting for other factors, including reported data by region, until a sensibly articulated pattern of loss was deduced and established.

My career as a forensic accountant was up and running. Through these and other early cases, I learned a lot about intellectual curiosity, keeping an open mind, establishing the facts and analysing the evidence. A logical and methodical approach was required to tell the story of what had happened based on what was known, and to project what would have happened 'but for' events (i.e. the destruction of war, the outbreak of mastitis, or some other change, which impacted the anticipated flow of things).

Indeed, the parallels to Holmes and his capacity for deductive and logical reasoning were fundamental to the nascent forensic mindset I was beginning to develop.

The Fraud Triangle

So far, so good, and I had enjoyed the accounting cases I had been involved in, but I wasn't quite following in the footsteps of my detective hero yet. Fortunately, my first fraud investigation was just around the corner.

In 1998, I was involved in a case involving possible irregularities in financial records. The company's bank statements appeared to reconcile, but there were an unusually high number of adjustments to customer accounts and a series of complex journal entries at the end of each month. No funds appeared to have gone missing, but a couple of obscure customers seemed to be taking an unusually long time to pay invoices, and there had been an increase in bad or irrecoverable debts.

Our team was deployed to understand the organisational structure, obtain and review relevant financial and other documentation, focus on transactions in key bank statements, customer accounts, and journal entries, and conduct interviews with the relevant staff. Observation, analysis and deduction were required, and the fact pattern was established.

This, I discovered, turned out to be a classic *'teeming and lading fraud'* or effectively *'stealing from Peter to pay Paul'*.

Essentially, a staff member received a customer payment, in this case by cheque, which was diverted into their own account instead of being deposited into the customer account. A carousel was then established involving the allocation of payment from Customer B into the account of Customer A, in order to balance the books and ensure the debt was not outstanding for any significant period of time, whilst hiding the original shortfall, which had effectively been misappropriated by a staff member with access to both payments and the ability to post accounting entries between customer accounts.

A payment received from Customer C was then applied to the account of Customer B, and so on until amounts were written off as bad debts, and/or other accounting balances were adjusted by journal entries, both of which occurred in this case. The number of customer accounts impacted and the series of complex journal entries affecting other accounting records effectively obfuscated the core transactions for a while, but as complexity increased, so did the questions.

Our team unravelled the series of transactions, adjusted for inappropriate journal entries, recorded the correct payments against the correct customer accounts, and presented the evidence in an interview to the staff member responsible. In total, more than

£100,000 had been misappropriated over a 16-month period, and the evidence was irrefutable.

It was on this case that I was first introduced to the model of the fraud triangle based on the work of the criminologist, Dr Donald R Cressey. The fraud triangle outlines the three conditions that typically lead to higher instances of occupational fraud:

- The *opportunity* to commit fraud, often due to weak internal controls or lack of oversight;
- The motive or *incentive* to commit fraud, often from personal financial problems or work-related issues, or simply the result of personal greed or addiction; and
- The *rationalisation* of why it is justifiable to commit fraud and not see it as wrong, a key differentiator between those who follow through and commit fraud and the rest of the population.

Cressey's research concluded that the presence of all three elements creates a fertile ground for fraud to occur.

In this case, all three components of the fraud triangle were present:

- The perpetrator had *opportunity* through unrestricted access in the finance department to both receive and allocate payments to customer accounts, as well as the ability to process journal entries in the accounting system;
- There was *incentive* to commit fraud as a result of a recent divorce, which resulted in money being tighter than had previously been the case; and
- The perpetrator was able to *rationalise* that the misappropriation was justifiable, given he had been with the organisation for a long period of time and had been passed over for promotion.

Fraudsters often don't regard themselves as having done anything wrong and see themselves in the same way we do, so they rationalise and explain, and look for others to blame. In my experience, these factors in combination are common when investigating the root causes of fraudulent activity and are features of the profile of the typical fraudster.

So, having channelled my inner Holmes to shine a light on the dark side for the first time, I was now ready to tackle one of the most meaningful and impactful cases in my career.

The Volcker Commission

The Volcker Commission, also known as the Independent Committee of Eminent Persons (ICEP), was established in 1996 to investigate funds held in dormant accounts in Swiss banks since the end of World War II. The Committee was headed by the former United States Chairman of the Federal Reserve, Paul Volcker, and was composed of three representatives from the Swiss Bankers Association and three representatives appointed by Jewish organisations.

Due to Switzerland's status as a neutral country on the border of Germany and Austria, many Jews, amongst others, fleeing persecution, deposited large amounts of money and valuables in various Swiss banks. However, when survivors or heirs of victims tried to recover their money following the war, many faced bureaucratic stonewalling by the banks, which often failed to account for the exceptional circumstances experienced by Holocaust victims and their families.

By the 1990s, it became clear that growing criticism of the behaviour of Swiss banks in relation to their handling of dormant accounts, most of which were presumed to have belonged to victims of the Holocaust, required a more robust response.

The Committee appointed PwC as one of five independent accounting firms to investigate some 254 Swiss banks covering a period of over 60 years from 1933 to 1995. In total, more than 4.1 million bank accounts had been open or opened in the period 1933 to 1945, and there were no remaining records for some 2.8 million additional accounts.

The account names, addresses and other details were compared with the names of known Nazi victims drawn from lists held by Holocaust researchers, and a second selective non-automated examination was undertaken on an account-by-account basis from other available documentation.

The work was painstaking, laborious and mundane, often requiring long hours deep in the vaults of the banks, with examination and analysis of old 1930s Swiss German banking records being compared with lists of names and other background details for matching purposes. Some were clear, many were not, but a comprehensive criteria and categorisation was required and deployed to establish connection and ownership.

The underlying weight of what we were doing, and what had happened to so many desperate families, was a driving force to bring justice wherever possible to the rightful heirs. The Swiss banks had often refused to release funds, citing banking secrecy laws and confidentiality requirements, leading to difficulties for claimants in proving a connection to the original depositor and ultimately rightful ownership.

In addition, the Nazi's systematic destruction of records, the lack of documentation available to survivors of concentration camps, and the lack of death certificates for Holocaust victims further complicated the claims process, as Swiss banks often required proof of death in order to release funds.

The emotional desire to match records was powerful, but the integrity of the process was of paramount importance, particularly as not all claimants were genuine, and some fraudulent and opportunistic claims had been made in the aftermath of World War II.

The Volcker Commission ultimately identified more than 50,000 Swiss bank accounts, which likely belonged to victims of the Holocaust, categorised as: Category 1, matched to the names of known Holocaust victims; Category 2, probable relationship between the account holder and Nazi persecution; or Category 3 and 4, which had a weaker nexus to the Holocaust.

By early 2020, the Volcker Commission had paved the way for the distribution of approximately US$1.29 billion of disbursements to over 450,000 claimants, including Jewish individuals and organisations, as part of a broader effort to address the financial losses suffered by victims of Nazi persecution.

My Values

My time in Switzerland had been important, but I was ready to return to London.

I had met a girl, Sally, who would go on to become my wife, and I wanted to spend more time with her. I was also enjoying the best of London, living initially in Walthamstow because it was cheap (I am Scottish after all), and then Fulham because it was time to up my game. I loved the vibrancy and abundance of London, and was determined to make the most of my time in the city with frequent visits to the museums, theatres and sporting arenas of the capital.

It was also here that my passion for travel was sparked by the many Antipodeans I came across on their two-year pilgrimage to London as a base to *'work hard, play hard,'* and spend their hard-earned cash on long weekends in Paris, Stockholm, Milan, wherever, often in consecutive weekends. To a conservative Scot, Europe was a one-off annual summer holiday, but this myth was blown away, first by envy, then by emulation. I was also embarrassed that they had often already been to more places in Scotland than I had, despite my 25-year head start.

I also enjoyed learning from the people I was working with in London: the Partners who were awesome in their depth of knowledge and experience; my mentors, who guided me through my initial forays; and my peers and fellow travellers, also making their way through the early stages of a career in Forensic.

I was learning and experiencing so much and soaking it all up like a sponge. I reflected on who I wanted to be, what my values were, and how the man in the mirror looked when I applied a forensic lens to my life. My values wouldn't be fully formed for some time yet, but I would ultimately alight around some core values, which really resonated with me, and have been a useful filter for decision-making when applied to the jobs, roles or tasks I was asked to do, and the dilemmas I would inevitably face in my daily life.

As my values, I've adopted MARTIN as an acronym: Meaningful, Authentic, Reflective, Team-impact, Integrity, and Natural. I'll explore these in more detail in future chapters, but, in summary, the questions I ask myself in relation to what I do are as follows:

- Is it *Meaningful*? Not everything has to have such a strong, clear purpose as the work on the Volcker Commission, but I do want what I do to have a positive, meaningful, purpose and impact;
- Is it *Authentic*? I want to be true to myself and what I do to genuinely align with my core beliefs, feelings, thoughts and sense of identity;
- What is my *Reflection?* I have periodically kept a journal over the years to be able to reflect on my experiences, particularly useful when I get things wrong and there are things to learn;
- What is the *Team-impact*? I want what I do to have a positive impact on other people, whether family, friends, colleagues or others I work with or in the community;
- Is there *Integrity*? I want who I am and what I do to have integrity and to be consistently aligned with my values; and

- Is it *Natural*? I want who I am to be instinctive and natural, and to align with my natural strengths and capabilities as I apply my forensic mindset to whatever comes my way.

As a clarifying and hopefully fun exercise, I encourage you to look through the list of values and attributes in Appendix 1 of this book, and pick and mix the ones that really resonate as guiding principles and personal values for you and how you want to live your life.

In recent years, as my forensic mindset and values have developed, I have found these to be instrumental to building professional health, wealth and happiness in my life, and I hope that you may find a similar approach to be helpful to yours too.

CHAPTER 3

OLYMPIC GOALS

"You got to try and reach for the stars or try and achieve the unreachable"

Cathy Freeman

A Land Down Under

My earliest memories of Australia came from the 1980s TV, music, and sport. Men at Work were the first to burst onto the scene with their iconic classic "Down Under" (and who could forget the classic rhyming couplet of "chunder" and "thunder"), followed by the *Crocodile Dundee* movies, and the introduction of a weekly highlights package of Aussie Rules football on Channel 4.

There was nothing subtle about Australian culture in those days. Next came *Neighbours* and the Scotts and Charlenes of Ramsay Street presented a gentler, middle-class aspirational suburbia, where the sun always shone, and life seemed pleasant. INXS became my favourite band, and their new wave rock became the dominant sound of our school's final year common room.

Still, Australia seemed a long way away, and it was. I didn't know anyone who had been to Australia, and I assumed that anyone who did would be gone forever.

As the 1990s rolled on, visiting Australia didn't seem quite so impossible. People I knew organised two-year secondments to Sydney and Melbourne, and young Aussies came to the UK in what seemed to be one colossal mutual exchange programme.

In 1997, I had my first experience of Australia when the opportunity came up to spend three months in sunny Darwin in my last act before moving to Forensic in London. Known for its tropical climate and constant temperatures of 30 degrees or higher (the seasons are simply 'Wet' and 'Dry', depending on rainfall and humidity), Darwin is the capital of the Northern Territory, an area almost six times the size of the UK but with less than 1% of the UK's population.

The office had one major audit client in a specialist sector, and they needed an audit in-charge. As the audit busy season was underway in the major centres of Sydney and Melbourne (more than a four-hour flight away), no one could be spared for three months. The clarion call went out to London and then, for some peculiar reason which will always be a mystery to me, Glasgow. Fortuitously, I had a gap in my schedule as I was planning my own move to London, so I jumped at the chance.

Darwin was an amazing experience. The work was fine, the people were friendly, and the extra-curricular attractions eye-opening.

I had my first experience of a 'jumping crocodile cruise', a very close encounter with some of nature's most fearsome predators, soaring through the air to trap raw meat dangled from a rope with jaw-dropping precision. I visited the stunning Kakadu and Litchfield national parks, with their abundant wildlife, waterfalls, wetlands and Aboriginal landmarks, as well as termite mounds taller than people.

I also loved the Aussie humour, reflected in the blunt simplicity of the adverts (*"if you drink and drive, you're a bloody idiot"*), and the local custom of measuring distance by beer consumption along notoriously straight highways (*"it's a six-pack to Katherine but a twelve-pack to Tennant Creek"*). Darwin is also the only place I have ever been breathalysed in a pub, as the authorities sought to persuade locals to temper consumption and/or take a taxi home.

I loved my time in Darwin, and having visited Cairns, Melbourne and Sydney on holiday on the way home, I knew this would be a great place to live for a while. Sydney, in particular, left a lasting impression with its stunning harbour, bridge and opera house, and the buzz around the city even then was building towards the new millennium, and the excitement of the forthcoming Olympic Games in 2000.

Dreamtime

In 1999, my dream opportunity knocked with the chance to spend two years on secondment with PwC's Forensic team in Sydney. After interviews and much form-filling to prove we were a 'de facto' couple, Sally and I grasped the opportunity. We arrived in Australia on sponsored business temporary resident visas on 15 September 1999, exactly one year to the day from the Opening Ceremony of Sydney 2000.

Cathy Freeman, the Aboriginal Australian 400m athlete, became the face of that Opening Ceremony and subsequently the Games. The Olympic torch passed through the hands of six Australian Olympic legends, including Dawn Fraser, Betty Cuthbert and Debbie Flintoff-King, before being passed to Cathy to light the Olympic Flame. She carried the hopes and expectations of a proud sporting nation. The pressure must have been intense.

Freeman was a groundbreaking athlete who transcended her sport in numerous ways. She was the first Aboriginal Australian to become a Commonwealth Games gold medallist, in the 4 x 100m relay, at the age of 16 in 1990. She subsequently won silver at the 1996 Olympics and gold at the 1997 and 1999 World Championships. By 2000, at the age of 26, she was in her prime.

She was also an important figure of reconciliation for a nation coming to terms with a sometimes-chequered past. The *Native Title Act 1993* had recognised the native title rights of Aboriginal and Torres Strait Islander peoples, overturning the doctrine of 'terra nullius', by which settlers had argued that the land of Australia was essentially unoccupied or uninhabited.

At the Sydney Olympics, Cathy's iconic gesture of carrying both the Australian and the Aboriginal flags, resonated with growing national reconciliation efforts across the country. Her profile as the face of the Sydney Games to the world, both in lighting the Olympic flame and winning a gold medal in the 400m, resonated deeply with Australians, helping foster national unity, and establishing her as an inspiring role model for her people.

Freeman's achievements, as an Aboriginal Australian of the Kuku-yalanji and Birri-gubba peoples, established her as a symbol of reconciliation for a maturing and increasingly confident nation on the world stage. She inspired countless Australians of all backgrounds, encouraging them to pursue their dreams, and later established the Cathy Freeman Foundation to advance Indigenous education and opportunity. In Aboriginal culture, the Dreamtime has a special resonance as it refers to a sacred time of creation when ancestral spirits formed the world in a continuous interconnected existence, encompassing the past, present and future.

As my journey continued in Australia, some investigation of the past also helped to inform my future.

The Hard Yards

The saying *"every journey begins with a single step"* is a well-known proverb, often attributed to the Chinese philosopher, Lao Tzu. Even the most ambitious or complex task, such as winning an Olympic gold medal, starts with a simple foundational action. And action is always required.

My task was much more modest, but I knew I needed to start training. I did technical training in the valuation of businesses, shares and other equities, the principles of litigation support, the assessment of damages, a graduate diploma in applied finance and investment, and the role of the forensic accountant as an expert witness.

I completed forensic investigation training, studied police interviewing techniques, the use of forensic technology, and the law around chain of custody and evidential integrity and admissibility. I also attended 'soft skills' courses on sales, negotiation, influencing, rapport building, presenting and communications.

In my spare time, I read Stephen Covey's *Seven Habits of Highly Effective People*, Dale Carnegie's *How to Win Friends and Influence People*, and occasional editions of the *Harvard Business Review*.

I was fortunate to be in a firm that provided such opportunities, but I was also curious and motivated to get better and set aside the time and focus to do the work. The disciplines that Freeman needed to be the best she could be, which was ultimately a world champion and Olympic gold medallist, were also required for me to be the best version of myself as a professional. As Warren Buffett said, *"the most important investment you can make is in yourself,"* and I was motivated to invest in my abilities.

I also learned through the projects I was on, most often the ones that didn't go so well.

Early in my time in Sydney, I worked on a difficult audit negligence case, which really challenged me. It was a complex international accounting standards case, in a sector where I had no prior experience, in an area I hadn't previously audited. I was also a relatively new Manager, working directly for a vastly experienced former Audit Partner, who just happened to be six foot four inches tall, with quite an intimidating reputation. The office of the late 1990s wasn't a place for the faint-hearted.

Known to bellow *"horsesh*t"* at report drafting that wasn't up to the mark, he took great delight in red pen elimination of paragraphs and pages of what I had thought were reasonably well-crafted analysis and argument. Deadlines were tight, hours were long, the learning curve was steep, and the fear factor was huge.

On many an occasion, he literally cut (with scissors) and pasted (with Sellotape) sections of the report into new and interesting sequences. We clearly didn't think alike, and I couldn't get on the same page (much of my drafting didn't even make the page!). I also self-sabotaged, obsessing over details that turned out not to be important, missing things that were, and failing to speak up when I was clearly struggling. I didn't have the experience or ability to do what he thought I should be able to do, so I retreated into my shell.

The report was ultimately done on time and on point, but the journey to get there was torturous. I had made several mistakes, both of omission (not owning up to, and then trying to paper over, my lack of relevant experience, knowledge and capabilities), and commission (errors of judgment, analysis and drafting, trying to do it all on my own, and not supporting my junior colleague). I should have been honest and asked for help. I should also have been true to myself, taken reasonable steps, supported my team better, and acted with more integrity. I had all my technical and developmental training, but I had failed on the job and needed to look in the mirror.

As Mike Tyson said, *"Everyone has a plan until they get punched in the face."* I felt I had been punched in the face and was struggling to get off the canvas.

I wish I had known then that *"99% of success is built on failure,"* according to Charles F. Kettering, the American engineer, who would ultimately (no doubt after a lot of failure), invent the electrical ignition system in cars, as well as the first aerial missile. I experienced my fair share of failure, or 'learning opportunities', around that time. I questioned myself whether I was in the right place, and made of the right stuff.

I wish I could say I came roaring back, but the truth was mostly one of perseverance, resilience and doing the hard yards until things slowly got better. I also found that I was learning, slowly, from working on a succession of projects with the same Partner. That learning may have cut deeper and been uncomfortable, but, in time, it led to more meaningful change.

As Cathy Freeman said, *"Success is not final, failure is not fatal: It is the courage to continue that counts."* With the benefit of hindsight, when projects were tough, I became better, and I kept going.

A little later, I worked on a series of contentious valuation disputes, including one in the mining sector, which turned on the disputed valuation of land, and whether it should include an option to renew leases. This required consideration of the legal definition of a 'lease' under tax law, the classifications that would prevent double taxation, whether options would be exercised, the value of intellectual property, and the appropriate interest rate to apply to calculate the net present value of estimated future income streams.

As I got more involved, my technical training and practical experience were beginning to pay off, and my muscle memory, modelling and speed of processing were developing. I was becoming fitter. It also helped that, on this one, I was working for the guy who had literally written the textbook, and had handed me a copy of it on Day 1 in Australia.

In 2001, another tax-related forensic accounting investigation began to dominate my time. With shades of the Enron scandal hitting the USA and wiping out Arthur Andersen globally around the same time, it essentially involved unravelling a complex series of inter-group transactions, which the Australian Tax Office alleged had no commercial rationale and appeared to have been entered into solely for the purpose of avoiding tax. The entity argued that interest expenses were legitimately incurred in the ordinary course of business, being the acquisition and holding of shares in another group entity, which would ultimately generate future tax assessable income in the form of dividends.

Notwithstanding these legal arguments, the role of the humble forensic accountant was to unwind this detailed series of transactions in relation to inter-group interest-bearing borrowings, principally by one group member, and the transfers of tax losses arising out of those borrowings to a number of other group members, then re-stating what the tax payable would have been 'but for' this series of transactions.

This was no small feat, given the nature, volume, and complexity of transactions between some 70 group entities over a six-year period. It ultimately required a sizeable team working for more than a year to complete and produce a report, including detailed appendices, which ran to more than 1,000 pages of analysis, with the potential difference in tax payable plus interest running into billions of dollars.

I didn't know it at the time, but this case would ultimately become one of the largest and longest-running tax disputes in Australian corporate history. Indeed, it would still be going for many years after I had left Sydney, and I would occasionally be contacted by the team who took it on with clarifying questions on the analysis I had done at the time.

It certainly taught me the importance of perseverance, focus, and attention to detail in the face of complex challenges. It also taught me to consistently follow through on the impact of decisions in every aspect of the work, as one small change in the treatment of transactions in one entity, had to be meticulously and consistently followed through in exactly the same manner to every other entity and the calculation of tax updated accordingly.

Those attributes of perseverance, focus and consistency were true for me as I did the hard yards, and were equally true for Cathy Freeman in her quest to become an Olympic champion.

Running my Race

In her athletics career, Cathy Freeman had to overcome a number of obstacles to achieve her Olympic dream. Between 1991 and 1997, she suffered from serious asthma, and whilst she had success along the way, there were also several setbacks, notably finishing fourth at the World Championships in Sweden in 1995, when she was a medal favourite, and then as a silver medallist behind France's Marie-José Pérec at the 1996 Olympics.

She also faced the pressure of expectation but took ownership of it, saying, *"I think the greatest amount of pressure is the pressure I place on myself."* As the form favourite, home favourite and face of Sydney 2000, that pressure reached new heights as she was again expected to face off with Pérec.

In the Olympic final, all that perseverance, dedication and training came to fruition as she ran the race of her life to win the 400m gold medal in a time of 49.11 seconds, becoming only the second ever Aboriginal Australian Olympic champion. After the race, as Australia revelled in her success, she took the applause of the crowd on her victory lap, carrying both the Aboriginal and Australian flags, as the crowning moment of her career. She had risen to the occasion, and her story was an inspiration to me, the nation and the world.

In a much smaller way, I had my own personal race to run almost 12 months later. After 2 years in Sydney, I had the opportunity to progress to Senior Manager in the team. All I had to do was pass a panel interview with a couple of Partners in the team. This was daunting, as I hadn't sat an interview in almost 10 years. I had to present the business case (why another Senior Manager was needed) and my personal case (why I was the right person for the job), as well as answer a series of questions.

I studied hard, setting out the reasons, the rationale and the activities that had led me to this point. I had to perform in the moment. My mindset was right, and my practice had been thorough. I leaned on the meaningful work I had done, the integrity I had shown, and the contributions I had made to the practice, both technical and team-oriented.

I had also run a business development initiative for lawyers over the past 2 years called *'Down at the Bar'*, which was basically a fun lawyer-themed quiz night (and, yes, I know how dull that sounds!). That helped me build confidence as a presenter and relationships with my peers in the law firms around town, even leading to regular 5-a-side Soccer Sundays as a 'guest player' with one of the firms. I felt I had a good story to tell and had done the hard yards of preparation.

The interview began, I hit my stride, kept a steady pace, managed not to stumble with any of the tough questions, and kept my eye on the finish line. The interview went well, and a week later, it was confirmed – I would be promoted to Senior Manager.

Reaching the Stars

Cathy Freeman reached the stars when she won her Olympic gold medal in September 2000.

In my personal life, I reached for stars almost exactly 12 months later in September 2001. On a cool spring evening at Bathers Pavilion in Balmoral, Sydney, I asked Sally to marry me. She said yes. I felt like an Olympic Champion. I was 29 years old and life could not have been better… but things were about to change….

Meeting Australian Prime Minister John Howard
at the Young Leaders Forum in Sydney, 2001

**Coming full circle and becoming an Australian citizen
(with dual nationality) in Mornington, 2024**

CHAPTER 4

CURIOUSITY AND COURAGE

"Be less curious about people and more curious about ideas."

Marie Curie

Homeward Bound

After two years in Sydney, we now had a wedding to plan. Sally and I also had to decide how long we would stay in Australia. The easy decision was to extend the timeframe of the initial two-year secondment, but our 'honeymoon period' of living in Australia couldn't go on forever, and many conversations were had over long walks and lazy dinners in relation to where we would ultimately call home. It was clear that when we flew to the UK, we were going "home"; equally, when we returned to Sydney, we were also going "home." It was nice to have two homes, but we needed to decide which home we would live in.

On the one hand, we loved Australia: the warmer climate, the familiar, easy-going culture, the vast and varied landscapes, and the quality of life, all of which seemed to blend the best of historic

Britain and modern America. On the other hand, we also missed the UK: family and friends, the uniquely British sense of humour, proximity to diverse European cultures, and a more intimate connection to what was happening in the world.

The events of September 11 2001, just one week after we got engaged, really brought it home. This was our JFK moment, as everyone remembers where they were when they heard the news. We had followed our normal daily commute regime: buy *The Australian* newspaper; catch the bus from Mosman over the bridge into the city; start with the sports section and make my way from back to front.

It was only when Sally caught a glimpse of the front cover that we began to process the full horror of what had happened in New York, Washington, DC and elsewhere in the USA. A truly shocking day, which brought (almost) all of humanity together. It was a day to be close to family and friends, yet here we were 12,000 miles away.

On the other hand, September 11 2001, illustrated what was different for us because it was the *one* event in all of our time in Sydney that directly and impactfully confronted our consciousness of the wider world. According to Quora, approximately 90% of all media news is negative, so from an Australian perspective, whilst bad things happen in the world, these are mostly elsewhere, far away, and the sun still shines outside our window. In that sense, being less connected to the world could be a good thing.

By Christmas 2001, our wedding plans were coming together, but the longer term was still unresolved.

In January 2002, all that changed with the devastating news that my mother's cancer, which had been in remission, had returned and was resistant to treatment. After much deliberation and agonising, and some exploratory calls back to London, it became clear that events had tipped the balance towards returning to the UK. The clincher was the possibility of returning to Edinburgh rather than London, and being 40 miles, rather than 400 miles, away from "home". A few hastily arranged interviews later, we decided that our flights home to get married would, in fact, become a one-way trip, and the next chapter in our story would be played out in Scotland.

In March 2002, we boarded a flight after two and a half amazing years in Sydney with memories, marriage and, if truth be told, some mild trepidation in mind. We were now homeward bound.

Home and Away

In April 2002, Sally and I were married at Auchincruive Estate in Ayrshire, Scotland. It was an amazing day of sunshine and celebrations with family and friends. A day for parents, siblings and extended family and friends from Scotland, England, Germany and Australia.

We were 30 years old. Mark brought the rings and delivered a punchy Best Man speech, and Sally's bridesmaid provided every support she could hope for in her oldest and dearest friend. The Bagpiper accompanied us from ceremony to sunshine, and from first dance to final fireworks as we left the reception. The day was everything we could ever have wanted it to be.

After honeymoon trips to the fjords and ice floes of Norway (after an Aussie summer, we were happy to explore a colder climate), and the dazzling delights of the South of France, we were ready to embark on our new married life in Edinburgh.

Scotland's capital city is an absolute gem. It is often referred to as the Athens of the North, with the imposing Castle Rock, which dominates the city skyline, reminiscent of the Athenian Acropolis, and the National Monument of Scotland on Calton Hill being modelled on the Parthenon. Indeed, the seven hills around which Edinburgh was built evoke comparisons with Ancient Rome, another nod to classical antiquity. Home to the historic Old Town and Royal Mile, which runs from the Castle to Holyrood Palace, the elegantly planned Georgian New Town, the rugged Salisbury Crags and Arthur's Seat, with breathtaking views over the city to the Forth of Firth and beyond, we were excited that Edinburgh was to be our new home.

And one of our first tasks as a married couple was to buy our first home. We had four months' grace whilst renting a room from a family friend, so, in the midst of a housing boom, my forensic mindset was fully engaged in reviewing properties, organising viewings, and crunching the numbers.

We viewed over 100 properties in three months, and I maintained a running spreadsheet of prices, values, pros, and cons before we finally settled on a charming Victorian one-bedroom top-floor apartment in Newington, two miles from the city centre, with views over the lovely Pentland Hills to the south of the city.

It was also time to get back to work, and I felt at home but also away from home. It was familiar – I was still with PwC, in Forensic, and back in Scotland, where it had all begun. Many of my cohort who started with me, as well as Partners and PAs, were still around. However, it was also different as the people I knew were in Glasgow or London, and I knew no one in the Edinburgh office.

The Scotland Forensic practice was essentially a start-up. A gregarious Edinburgher I had worked with in London, had set up the practice around 6 months earlier, but left a month after I joined. He had just recruited a newly qualified accountant from Audit around the same time I started, so within weeks, it was 2 newbies against the world as we tried to establish a brand-new practice in a new market.

The other idiosyncrasy was that my boss was in Belfast. A quirk of the merger between Price Waterhouse and Coopers & Lybrand was that the Northern Ireland offices retained operational independence as a geography rather than adopting the service line model of the rest of the UK firm. As a result, the Northern Ireland firm could invest in areas of consulting at lower thresholds than the UK firm, which ultimately included a start-up Forensic practice in Scotland.

It was weird to be employed by and reporting to a different division than all my other colleagues, and flying to Belfast every other month. On the other hand, given the history of the Troubles in Northern Ireland, an extra three days' public holiday came my way each year. Whilst I wasn't going to be celebrating St. Patrick's Day or marching in the Orange Walk, it was definitely nice to be out of the office for an extra few days each year.

Curiosity and Kindness

Curiosity can be defined as the desire to know or learn about something. It is a fundamental human quality, that drives exploration, investigation and learning. It encourages us to ask questions, seek information and broaden horizons, which is essential for personal development and understanding the world around us. It is also a fundamental quality in developing an effective forensic mindset.

In my new role, I had to be curious. I was effectively leading a nascent Forensic practice in Scotland with neither template nor tutor to guide me. The majority of my experience had been in Disputes & Expert Witness work, but it would have been a brave lawyer to hire a 30-year-old Senior Manager as a quantum expert on their litigation. I had also run a number of fraud and financial investigations, but it was tough to drum up business unless a client had experienced a fraud that week. We would be needed urgently or, in most cases, not at all. This was my first exposure to the need for real business development, and it was a steep learning curve.

I spent a lot of time asking questions of senior Partners and Directors around me and offering to help with anything I could. I studied topics of relevance to forensic accounting and read the business papers for angles of interest. I borrowed the best forensic thought leadership from around the country and put a Scottish spin on it for the local market. I offered to come to client meetings, speak at internal team meetings and external events, and generally put myself about. I went to Aberdeen, Glasgow and Edinburgh, meeting with clients, lawyers and teams in each market. In summary, I made a nuisance of myself, no doubt blundering at times, but with a desire to understand, learn and make a success of this.

And slowly but surely, success would come. Some proactive advice on fraud risk frameworks here, some limited investigation work there. One of my first projects was to interview a suspect in Dundee who had allegedly stolen £13,000. I realised then the impact of a smart suit, a sombre expression, and the fear factor when the "investigator" comes to interview. He very quickly crumbled in a bundle of nerves, confessed to everything, and explained in detail what he had done and how he had done it. He wrote a cheque at the end of the meeting for the full £13,000, driven no doubt by a forlorn hope that repayment would save his job and avoid having to confess to his wife and family. Fraud is not a victimless crime, and the cascading impact can flow far and wide.

Other early wins required some deeper, more persistent curiosity like the investigation of dormant pension accounts of customers who had 'gone away' (i.e. allegedly moved away with no forwarding address), but had ultimately been raided by a clerk who had temporarily changed bank account details and diverted funds on a very specific sub-category of dormant accounts, which only he controlled, and which met certain specific criteria that would minimise the chances of arousing suspicion.

Or the teeming and lading fraud conducted by the finance team member who systematically stencilled an extra "1" onto certain cheques, which would be diverted into his account to cover his gambling addiction, whilst diligently ensuring that the correct payments and accounting entries were made elsewhere so the supplier accounts as a whole were always in balance.

Both frauds had been multi-year, intricate schemes that had evaded previous internal audit reviews and diverted hundreds of thousands of pounds into the hands of the perpetrators. Successful investigation and resolution of these cases really helped build my confidence and reputation within the firm, and curiosity, persistence, and questioning were fundamental to doing so.

Curiosity was also important in my personal life in 2002, as I was acutely aware of my need to be curious about cancer. My Mum had first been diagnosed with breast cancer at the tender age of 47 in 1995. A small lump, one-quarter the size of a fingernail, had been discovered in her breast. After initial exploration, she was treated with radiotherapy, which appeared to remove the lump, and then Tamoxifen to impede the impact of high oestrogen levels and prevent recurrence.

At each quarterly check-up, she appeared to be in the clear and then came off Tamoxifen, as expected and hoped for, after 5 years. However, appearances had been deceptive, and some cancerous cells, which had been lurking in the lining off her lung, re-emerged in 2000 once the masking effects of Tamoxifen were no longer applied. This was a new and trickier stage of development, and whilst more invasive treatments, including chemotherapy, had initially been effective in controlling the cancer, by early 2002, it was clear that it would ultimately be incurable.

Around this time, I started reading about Marie Curie, the name behind many cancer and palliative care centres in the UK. Born in Warsaw in 1867, she moved to Paris in 1891 to continue her scientific work, subsequently marrying French physicist Pierre Curie, with whom she ultimately won a Nobel Prize in Physics for their pioneering work in developing the theory of radioactivity.

Marie Curie also became the first person to ever win two Nobel Prizes, adding a Nobel Prize in Chemistry for the discovery of two new elements, radium and polonium (named after the country of her birth), using techniques, that she had invented. In World

War I, she also developed mobile radiography units to provide X-ray services to field hospitals, bringing more accurate diagnoses and preventing unnecessary amputations. Her pioneering work revolutionised oncology and laid the foundation for radiation therapy as the cornerstone for cancer treatment. The work of Marie Curie had been vital to the treatment now helping my Mum.

Marie Curie famously described her *"spirit of curiosity"* as *"indestructible,"* and she pursued her work with relentless resolve. She faced many prejudices as a woman of science at the turn of the 20th Century, but never gave up, her work ethic, perseverance, dedication and determination to understand the forces of nature driving her on.

She was famously *"more curious about ideas than people,"* saying that *"nothing in life is to be feared, only to be understood."* Her determination propelled her on to develop the theory of radioactivity, explaining how atoms decay, and to discover new elements, which helped alleviate pain for countless people in subsequent generations. Her story, as portrayed by Rosamund Pike in the 2019 film *Radioactive*, is inspirational and shows what can be achieved with curiosity and commitment.

I was certainly grateful that her discoveries had helped to alleviate pain for Mum in what was a difficult time. Our family grew closer as Mum, who had been the centrifugal force for all of us through the consistency of her love, kindness, care, and dedication, faced her ultimate battle. We did our best to support her and one another, but it was hard when someone who had loved us unconditionally throughout our lives was breaking down before us.

Courage of Knowledge

Another film on the life of Marie Curie, *The Courage of Knowledge*, explores her dedication to her work and family following the death of her husband in a tragic accident, and it was these twin attributes of curiosity and courage that I relied on during our first few years in Edinburgh.

Some local cases involved investigating tax evasion and the discovery of 2 sets of accounting records in a wholesale cash and carry business with some dubious characters as 'suppliers' in the background.

Other cases required assessment of the consequential loss arising as a result of compulsory purchase and relocation by government of each of a furniture store, a bakery, and a retail store, in the path of a planned new motorway extension through a commercial district of Glasgow. In each case, I had to establish the facts, analyse the evidence, and determine what the position would have been 'but for' these events. And to hold firm in the face of quite a bit of pressure to change my opinion.

As we proved our capabilities, the volume of work grew, as did the team, and from small acorns, we grew to 4, to 6 and ultimately to 8 people across Edinburgh and Glasgow. It was an exciting time.

We also went international with interesting fraud and corruption investigations for local clients at subsidiaries in Brazil, Germany, Singapore and the USA. Some intensive weeks were had in Sao Paolo, Bavaria, Singapore and California, uncovering: "marketing" schemes, which were ultimately bribes to customers; fraudulent kickbacks arising from collusion with suppliers; 2 sets of accounting records ("official" ones fabricated for reporting purposes, and "unofficial" ones detailing the true, often illegal, activities); and perhaps disappointingly, a suspected fraudulent mastermind whose accounting chaos derived from gross incompetence, rather than gross misconduct or misappropriation. Sometimes people really are just mad rather than bad.

One interesting case involved a trip to Cyprus to investigate suspected irregularities on a defence force base, and I definitely needed my courage for that one. I think I felt more intimidated than the people I was investigating, but, then again, they had access to guns.

International work also came to Scotland with a large Foreign & Corrupt Practices Act investigation in Aberdeen, which included reporting to US lawyers, the US Department of Justice and the UK Serious Fraud Office. This was a truly global investigation following a self-reporting disclosure to the US Securities & Exchange Commission (SEC), with lawyers in New York and London coordinating teams in Houston, Singapore and Aberdeen, on the hunt for instances of bribery and corruption of state officials in numerous countries and areas of operation, by a listed international technology company. The multi-million-dollar fine would have been significantly higher 'but for' the company's self-disclosure and deferred prosecution agreement given the company's cooperation, extensive remediation programme, and agreement to implement enhanced corporate compliance and reporting.

Finally, by mid-2004, I had found a lawyer willing to take a chance on me as an accounting expert. Other than some smaller quantum cases, this was my first real break, and it was to go all the way to expert evidence and cross-examination by a barrister in the Court of Session in Edinburgh. It involved a high-end restaurant on Edinburgh's Royal Mile, and the consequential loss suffered as a result of a period of forced closure.

As accounting expert, I was engaged to determine the quantum of loss, which required a detailed assessment of historic results, future projections, trading volumes, footfall, capacity constraints, pricing, and fixed and variable costs of the restaurant and its competitors, with a view to comparing actual results with my assessment of what they would have been 'but for' the closure.

I wrote my expert report, then a rebuttal of the other expert's report, and in our first 'meeting of experts', we tried to narrow the areas of disagreement between us. It became apparent that we were so far apart on quantum and the parties so entrenched in their positions, that this was heading straight to trial. And so it was that I was called into the witness box as accounting expert for the very first time, which was daunting, particularly as the other expert was almost twice my age and vastly more experienced.

Being an independent expert in court is a curious role. Experts are engaged by a law firm acting on behalf of their client, who ultimately pays the fees, but the overriding duty of the expert is to the court. Importantly, this included not the lawyer or the client. In the witness box, you swear an oath, and you are on your own. Everything in your report, your credibility, your expertise, and of relevance to the case (to the extent it can be made relevant to your opinion), is fair game for questioning.

And barristers are experts in questioning.

It can be daunting, but the key is to remain within, and never be drawn outside, the tramlines of your expertise.

I prepared so well. It may have been my first time, but I was determined to understand my report, the other expert's report, our joint expert report, our areas of disagreement, and the key evidence on which I had formed my opinion, inside and out, from every angle. It was like every exam I had ever faced, and I was truly forensic in the depth and detail I went to. I was as well prepared as I had ever been, and I had the courage of knowledge to truly be that expert I had sworn on oath to be.

After more than three hours of cross-examination in the highest court in the land, my job was done. All my preparation had been worthwhile, and with the exception of a couple of curly questions, I had survived, and I thought I had acquitted myself well.

A few months later, when the verdict came through, I felt more than vindicated. The presiding judge, Lord Johnston, in his Judgement said: *"The two reports produced by Mr Dougall...are immaculate in their presentation...Mr Dougall's verbal evidence to me was measured, calculated and totally balanced, and I have absolutely no hesitation in accepting everything he said to me in substance, as a matter of accuracy.... I have no hesitation, having listened to the witness, in accepting his evidence in its entirety."*

It was a win for curiosity and the courage of my convictions.

Closure

In June 2005, more than three years after we returned from Sydney, my mum passed away at home, surrounded by her loving family, at the tender age of 57. It was remarkable that she had been able to fight on for so long, having endured every treatment she could reasonably have undertaken. She had seen my sister Lynn and me both married, and Dad provided a loving environment to the very end. She was the safe space and the learning environment of my childhood, and the source of many of my redeeming qualities. She taught me curiosity, kindness and, in particular, courage, to the very end. I will always love her and remember her so very fondly.

CHAPTER 5

FOLLOW THE MONEY

"I have sworn to capture this man with all legal powers at my disposal, and I will do so."

Eliot Ness in *The Untouchables*

Behind every successful fortune, there is a crime

Originally attributed to French novelist Honore de Balzac, this was the line chosen by Mario Puzo as the epigraph of his best-selling novel *The Godfather*, which ultimately became one of the most successful movie trilogies of all time. And a personal favourite of mine.

I have been intrigued by the mafia since I first saw *The Godfather* films as a teenager in the 1980s. However, it is with that other mafia classic, *The Untouchables*, and the confrontation between the inimitable policeman Eliot Ness and Prohibition-era gangster Al Capone, that we start on the money trail. Indeed, the real story of

Al Capone's downfall truly begins with the little-known father of forensic accounting, Frank J. Wilson.

Wilson was born in Buffalo in 1887, and after training as an accountant and serving in World War I, he became the Chief New York State Investigator for the United States Food and Drug Administration. He then joined the United States Internal Revenue Bureau's Intelligence Unit. It was in this capacity that he would earn a reputation as a thorough investigator of tax returns and income, which ultimately led him to the Al Capone investigation.

Elmer L. Irey, who led the Bureau, said of Wilson that: *"He will sit quietly looking at books eighteen hours a day, seven days a week, forever, if he wants to find something in those books,"* and it was this rigour and perseverance that would lead him to the smoking gun that would ultimately prove to be Al Capone's downfall.

In 1929, an investigation by law enforcement agents, including Eliot Ness, into Prohibition-era bootlegging uncovered evidence that indicated Al Capone's brother, Ralph, had not paid income taxes on a sizable illegal income. As a result, the Intelligence Unit began to build a series of tax evasion cases against leading figures in the Chicago mafia, with the ultimate goal of convicting Al Capone.

Frank J. Wilson was appointed to lead the investigation into linking Al Capone to taxable income, and his team examined over two million documents and evidence acquired in several raids on Capone's establishments over a six-year period.

The strategy was to demonstrate that Capone spent significant sums of money, which was incompatible with having no discernible sources of income or wealth. Wilson and his men questioned merchants, real estate agents, proprietors, hotel clerks, bartenders, and accountants, many of whom were afraid of what might happen if they provided information on Capone. Despite offers of protection, they still refused to speak about their business with the gangster.

The team also analysed phone records, investigated banks and credit card agencies, and seized and reviewed accounting records, searching for any weak points in Capone's operations. Whilst Capone was smart in how he moved his money, and how and with whom he did business, Wilson was relentless and exceptionally thorough in his search for information. Even rumours that Capone had hired killers to assassinate Wilson could not deter him.

The breakthrough came when the Intelligence Unit identified a J.C. Dunbar, who had purchased $300,000 worth of cashier's cheques at a bank in Cicero. The Intelligence Unit worked out that his real name was Fred Ries and discovered that he was on the run and hiding in St. Louis, where he was found, arrested and returned to Chicago.

Wilson got Ries to testify that the cashiers' cheques represented gambling profits received by Capone's ally, Jake Guzik, and his testimony secured Guzik's conviction. The next breakthrough was the discovery of a ledger documenting financial records of a large gambling operation, with calculations of net income every few pages, which were typically divided between individuals, referred to only as A, R, and J in the ledgers, but crucially with an entry that read *"Frank paid $17,500 for Al."* This was Wilson's chance to link Capone to the income, but he still had to find where the money was held to convince a criminal jury that Capone was guilty beyond a reasonable doubt.

The goal was now to track down the bookkeepers and get them to testify that 'A' and 'Al' in the ledgers were references to Capone. Wilson spent weeks evaluating handwriting from every single one of Capone's associates, checking voter registers, bank deposits, bail bond certificates, and other documents. An informant helped Wilson identify a key bookkeeper in Miami, whom Wilson tracked down and persuaded to testify against Capone. The Intelligence Unit then identified monthly wire transfers from Capone to his family in Chicago, as well as wire transfers in Miami under an assumed name.

By 1931, the Intelligence Unit had finally pieced together all the evidence required to prosecute Capone, and a grand jury was convened to decide his fate. The result was that Capone was indicted on 23 counts of tax evasion of over $250,000 of income in the period 1924 to 1929. Capone was proven guilty, given an 11-year prison sentence and fined $300,000 in court costs, considered to be an astronomical sum for a tax evader at that time.

Capone ultimately served his sentence at the maximum security prison on Alcatraz, and after his release, he died in 1947. Without the determination, rigour and painstaking efforts of Wilson and his team, Capone's criminal activities could have gone on much longer, and he may never have been stopped.

Wilson subsequently went on to investigate the Lindbergh kidnapping in the 1930s, with sources indicating that his insistence on tracking the serial numbers on gold certificates used as ransom money, ultimately led to the arrest and conviction of Bruno Richard Hauptmann. He was also named chief of the Secret Service and, under his stewardship, the production and distribution of counterfeit money through a nationwide education program called "Know Your Money" was significantly curtailed by the time of his retirement in 1947. Through Wilson's long career, the disciplines and value of forensic accounting were well established, as was my path to start following in his footsteps some 50 years later.

By 2005, the great fortunes of the UK's richest people were quantified and presented in a much more systematic way in the annual publication of *The Sunday Times Rich List*. The movers, shakers, winners and losers, sliding snakes and ladder climbers were there for all to see. Our Tax team would take an interest in high-net-worth individuals and families who could benefit from efficient tax planning. However, with my sceptical, forensic mindset, I would look at it through a different lens. If someone had recently come into great wealth, what was the real secret behind their success? If it sounded too good to be true, could it be that it wasn't true?

Zooming out, I could see that in the case of someone like Trevor Baines, whose £130 million fortune once placed him alongside rock stars such as Eric Clapton and Phil Collins at 349th on the Rich List. However, by 2009, he had been convicted of taking part in a money laundering scam, involving false accounting and artificially inflated share prices.

Mario Puzo may not have been right that behind *every* great fortune there is a crime, but it was certainly true in some cases.

Leave the gun, take the cannoli

By 2006, these classic words from Clemenza in *The Godfather* became symbolic of a decision I had to make during a dawn raid on a suspected drug dealer's house in the West of Scotland. We had been instructed by the Crown Prosecutions Office to conduct a forensic accounting exercise under the *Proceeds of Crime Act 2002*, which essentially allowed law enforcement agencies to seize and confiscate assets obtained through criminal activities, and to combat money laundering. The Act allowed courts to issue Confiscation Orders against individuals convicted of crimes, requiring them to pay a sum equivalent to the financial benefits gained from their criminal activities, as well as civil recovery of assets from individuals who had not been convicted but who were suspected of benefitting from criminal conduct.

In this case, having completed all of our engagement and environmental risk checks, and being accompanied by a lawyer with a relevant court order, plus two reassuringly large policemen, we knocked on the door of the unsuspecting individual at 7:30 am. The named individual was not at home, but his wife and parents were, and after some initial shock, histrionics and colourful language (by them, not us), we were permitted entry. The two large policemen were certainly persuasive.

Our task was to conduct and appropriately document the search and seizure of anything on-site, which could reasonably be suspected of being funded as a result of the proceeds of crime. In this respect, two expensive watches were identified, as was more than £10,000 in cash located in a bedroom wardrobe. This was appropriately counted, checked, 'bagged and tagged' and prepared for removal from the premises.

A thorough search of the house was near completion when the named individual returned in a fit of fury. So much so that one of his few remaining teeth flew out of his mouth mid-rant, which he then proceeded to pick up and re-insert into his mouth. It had clearly been loose and had happened before. One of the policemen later suggested to me that he bore all the hallmarks of coming down from a drug high, possibly as a result of sampling his own produce.

Our 'cannoli' moment was a decision we had to make on whether or not to take possession of two racing greyhounds kennelled in the back garden. On the one hand, these could potentially be valuable, income-generating assets, purchased as a result of the proceeds of crime. On the other hand, where on earth were we going to house, feed, train, and look after two racing greyhounds, both of whom looked a little world weary, and who would take responsibility for them. Having carefully weighed the evidence and performed a quick cost-benefit analysis, we decided, on balance, to leave the dogs and take the cash.

There seemed to be several encounters on the edges of criminality around this time, most notably when assisting my colleagues across the water in Northern Ireland. In one such case, we had to review the integrity of the use of Government grant funding to certain social programmes in Belfast, which had potentially been siphoned off to organisations connected to paramilitary groups. The procurement process was somewhat less transparent and robust than would normally be expected, the suppliers more mysterious and less visible than usual, and the cost of services rendered seemed potentially high and uncompetitive in the market (or may have been but for the lack of alternative quotes). It was certainly interesting to be working in a corporate environment, but on the edges of something more sinister.

In another high-profile case, we had a role to play following one of the largest ever bank robberies in UK history. In the week before Christmas 2004, some £26.5 million in used and unused bank notes, was stolen from Northern Bank headquarters in Belfast by an armed gang during a raid in which family members of two bank officials were taken hostage. An independent review was urgently required to determine the value of the used and unused banknotes, which had gone missing as a result of the heist.

Whilst the Police Service of Northern Ireland investigated the crime, and the Independent Monitoring Commission, the British government, the Taoiseach in Ireland, and the Provisional Irish Republican Army pointed fingers and dealt with the political fallout, the bank needed to determine what had been stolen and a remediation plan to minimise its losses, which ultimately resulted in the replacement of its £10, £20, £50 and £100 notes, with new banknotes issued, with different colours, new logos and altered serial numbers. Although some £4.5 million in notes from other banks and £5.5 million in old, used Northern Bank notes, were untraceable, by March 2005, the £16.5 million of uncirculated banknotes, which had been stolen would be very hard to spend.

Great men are not born great, they grow great

This quote from Don Vito Corleone in *The Godfather* really resonates with me. It reflects the crucial role of personal development, integrity, experience, and choices in shaping and growing character over time.

However, sometimes the perception of "great men" can be misleading.

In 2005, the recently knighted Sir Fred Goodwin was seen as one of the great titans of British industry as the Chief Executive Officer (CEO) of the Royal Bank of Scotland (RBS), one of the largest and fastest growing banks in the world. Through aggressive expansion by acquisition, and ruthless cost-saving measures, the press had given him the moniker *'Fred the Shred'*, as he presided over the stunning rise of RBS to global prominence, which briefly led to it becoming the world's largest company by asset value (£1.9 trillion).

Only three years later, the party was over and, in the midst of the Global Financial Crisis, RBS was forced to rely on a UK Government financial rescue package, which resulted in the Government owning a majority of the shares, and Sir Fred Goodwin stepping down as CEO.

Some of the cultural issues, which ultimately led to the collapse of the bank, were illustrated in the case of the downfall of Donald Mackenzie, a Business Manager at a branch in Edinburgh, where he had been named Business Banking 'Manager of the Year' for three consecutive years from 2002-2004.

However, by 2005, his 'success' in generating business loans since 1999 had proven to be a sham, and he ultimately pled guilty to using loopholes in the loan approval system to inflate the value of these loans and defraud the bank of over £20 million. Mackenzie had accessed the money through the bank's loan system by setting up around 70 false accounts using bogus names, and then spent five years trying to cover his tracks by moving the money around using tens of thousands of transactions.

Mackenzie was finally caught after RBS introduced a new 'loan guard' computer system, which inadvertently crashed whenever customer data was amended during the loan process. It was during the process of identifying the bug that caused the system to crash, that the bank's IT department also stumbled upon the suspect data that had been entered into the system by Mackenzie. Another apparently 'great man' brought low and a further illustration of the maxim that if it sounds too good to be true, then maybe it is.

It was apparent that there had been a fundamental change in the culture of the bank, which had been operating since 1727, over a very short period of time. There had also been an aggressive domestic and international acquisition strategy, which had absorbed a number of larger financial institutions with different characteristics over a short period of time, and the integration strategy was struggling to cope with the differing size, complexity and IT systems of the various financial institutions coming into the group. These factors, coupled with aggressive cost-cutting measures, meant that some of the checks and balances, which had previously been in place, were no longer fit for purpose, and/ or the employees who had previously performed those roles were no longer there and had not been replaced. In the circumstances, RBS had been exposed to one of the largest ever frauds in Scottish corporate history.

By this point, after four years of building the Forensic practice in Scotland, I felt that the experience I had gained and the value I could add was growing. Those consistent, unglamourous disciplines of perseverance, resilience and determination to follow the methodology, establish the facts, analyse the evidence, and follow the money were now ingrained as essential building blocks to help me uncover the truth. There were no real shortcuts to building my experience and expertise, and my reputation would grow by doing the right things consistently. I had seen the pitfalls of greed and deception in some of the characters I had come across.

I was also learning practical lessons about leadership and management of people. One Partner talked about generosity of spirit, in leaders having a responsibility to share their most precious resources of time, experience and wisdom. Another talked not about being in charge, but in taking care of those in your charge. It was clear that leading people was becoming an increasingly important part of my role, and with eight people over two locations in Scotland, plus additional responsibilities in Northern Ireland, I was enjoying the experience of new challenges and opportunities to learn and develop. I certainly wasn't great, but I was growing.

It's not personal, Sonny, it's strictly business

With growth comes growing pains.

When Michael Corleone explains to his older brother in clear, rational terms why he, personally, has to take a more ruthless, calculated approach in *The Godfather*, he crosses the Rubicon from reluctant outsider to leader of the Corleone family business. He asserts the need to prioritise the success and survival of the family business above individual sentiment, and his separation of personal feelings from cold, calculated decisions in the interests of the family business sets him on a path that has implications for his future and for those around him.

In 2006, a decision by my boss to throw me under the proverbial bus for a failing on one of his engagements was a cold, calculated, strictly business, self-preservation decision on his part. It wasn't personal, but it had implications, particularly as it was just the latest in a number of actions that had eroded my trust in him. It ultimately led to me being withdrawn from a promotion process at the 11th hour, and despite support for me from Partners in London, Edinburgh and Belfast, the power dynamic and timing was such that I would have no choice but to wait for the next promotion cycle to go again. I would also have to continue working for him and with him. However, trust, once fundamentally broken, becomes irretrievable.

I worked on for several months in difficult circumstances and looked out for the interests of my team as best I could, but after 13 years with PwC, I had, for the very first time, come across someone I could not trust. Unfortunately, he was my boss, and I now felt that I had no alternative but to leave. In my case, the old maxim that people leave bosses, not companies, was true.

I'm gonna make him an offer he can't refuse

Over the following six months, I considered my options.

On a practical level, I had never had to prepare a professional CV for interview purposes before, as I was still at university the last time I had applied for jobs. However, the more I wrote down, the more impressive it sounded, so I took some confidence that maybe I did have some interesting and meaningful experience that would appeal to other potential employers.

I had thoroughly enjoyed working in a Big Four professional services firm, and the people I knew at the other firms spoke of a similar culture and experience to PwC. I also felt that I knew how they operated, so reasonably quickly I resolved to restrict my focus to the other three firms or to move internally within PwC.

In terms of Scotland, I knew my counterpart at KPMG, and had occasional catch-ups with him over the years as we joked about trying to recruit one another. However, KPMG already had a leader with a larger, more established team who had been in place for a number of years, so it wasn't clear that there would be an opening for me. Deloitte and EY had no real Forensic presence in Scotland at the time, so they were greenfield sites to potentially build again what I had done at PwC.

We were also potentially open to moving location. Scotland was a small market in terms of Forensic, and whilst we had moved from Sydney to Edinburgh for family reasons at the time, it was apparent that longer-term career opportunities in this specialist niche would be limited by the size of the market if we stayed in Scotland. I would either have to broaden my experience beyond Forensic to become useful in Scotland, or if I wanted to specialise in Forensic, I would probably have to move to a larger market.

We were now approaching our mid-30s and keen to have a family, so the thought of moving to London was prohibitive from a cost perspective. Upon leaving Sydney, we had committed to applying for Permanent Residency, so we had the option to return to Australia one day, but again, this was too big a move right now. We looked into opportunities in Europe, but the language barrier was prohibitive, apart from potential roles in Prague or Warsaw where English was the dominant business language at the time, and we looked into these briefly.

In the end, all three firms made me an offer to join as a Director: Deloitte and EY to build their new Forensic practice in Scotland; and KPMG to lead their existing Forensic practice in Manchester, reporting to a Partner who led the business across the North of England. KPMG ultimately played the Vito Corleone role, making me *The Godfather* offer, which I could not refuse, from both a financial and a career development perspective.

And so, at the end of 2006, I handed in my notice to PwC and we began to prepare for a new life, some 300 miles south in Manchester. We also had some good news to celebrate as Sally was now pregnant. 2007 would be a time of new beginnings....

CHAPTER 6

LEARNING TO QUARTERBACK

"I'm the best decision this organisation has ever made"

**Robert Kraft, owner of the New England Patriots,
attributed to Tom Brady**

The Best Decision

In 2000, an unheralded college quarterback was selected with the 199th pick of the NFL draft. His pre-draft scouting report read as follows: *"Poor build, skinny, lacks great physical stature and strength, lacks mobility and ability to avoid the rush, lacks a really strong arm, can't drive the ball downfield, does not throw a really tight spiral, system type player who can get exposed if forced to ad-lib, gets knocked down easily."*

As a result, 198 players were selected ahead of him that year, and virtually no one expected a stellar career when he was hired as a potential backup to starting quarterback Drew Bledsoe.

Tom Brady had confidence that he would be ready when he got his chance, and, unlike most low-drafted rookie players, he was willing to commit to the owner, in no uncertain terms, that the Patriots would not regret their decision.

I had no such confidence. However, I was determined that I would do everything in my power to ensure that KPMG did not regret their decision to invest in me. Like Tom Brady, I was ready and willing to work hard, understand my role, and learn from more experienced professionals ahead of me, a major reason for choosing the larger practice in Manchester over staying in Scotland. I was keen to be trainable, coachable, and hungry to learn so I would be ready and able to step into that leadership role when the time was right to do so.

I was also realistic. I arrived in Manchester knowing no one. Well, that wasn't strictly true, but the only people I did know were former colleagues of mine at PwC and Deloitte, who had recently hired a PwC Partner. With no prior history, it was a great opportunity to reinvent myself in a new firm, in a new city, in a new country from scratch.

Manchester proved to be a great place to do so, a fascinating city with a rich industrial heritage. Famous as one of the historic centres of the Industrial Revolution, the textile industry, and the birthplace of the worldwide co-operative movement, it felt like the second city of Britain. It was at the Midland Hotel in the city centre, where Mr Rolls first met Mr Royce in 1904, and the Rolls-Royce car company was formed. In more modern times, the vibrant music scene had spawned Oasis, Joy Division and The Stone Roses. By early 2007, the emerging sporting rivalry of the age was between the traditional footballing powerhouse of Manchester United, and the nouveau riche "noisy neighbours" of Manchester City. There was going to be a thriving cultural scene to explore here.

KPMG was organised as a regional hub across the North of England, encompassing the major cities of Manchester and Leeds, alongside smaller offices in Liverpool, Newcastle and Preston. Our Forensic team was just over 20 strong, and was led by a Senior Partner, who was relocating from Manchester to Leeds following my arrival. He was the only Partner in the region but was supported by four Directors: two in Leeds, including one now part-time in the swansong of his career; and a newly promoted Director in Manchester alongside me. I had been hired to lead the team in Manchester and, over time, there was a possibility to progress to Partner and a broader leadership role if things worked out.

One of our early opportunities justified the decision as the Partner won a significant engagement with a well-known car manufacturer, which had uncovered potential bribery and corruption issues across its operations in Scandinavia and Central and Eastern Europe. A major forensic technology data capture, analysis and investigation was required, in very tight deadlines, to identify potential instances of corruption and investigate key persons of interest.

The Partner's substantial prior experience of investigations, including working with lawyers, regulators and automotive clients, as well as his wider role as European region investigations leader, meant he was perfectly placed to lead this engagement and deploy a large international team covering multiple workstreams. I supported on one of those workstreams and led the team and engagement aspects of the work, whilst he focused on the technical and client handling aspects. We both played to our strengths, but it was fascinating to see him operate at close quarters on a significant, stressful and complex investigation with multiple stakeholders, including the Serious Fraud Office.

It was also insightful seeing him interact with clients and Partners, both in Manchester and Leeds, and in our quarterly reviews with national Forensic leadership. There are different things I have learned from all the leaders I have worked with, and from him, a meticulous attention to detail, and asking the follow-up, open, curious, probing question was almost always insightful. He was definitely the most forensic Forensic Partner I have ever worked with.

Meticulous attention to detail and learning from other professionals was also fundamental to Tom Brady's mindset, and after sitting on the bench for over a year, he finally had his opportunity when Drew Bledsoe was injured early in the 2001 season.

He was ready.

Despite low expectations, he excelled from the moment he replaced Bledsoe, leading the Patriots to victory in 14 of their remaining 17 games, including their first-ever Super Bowl win. He was also selected to the Pro Bowl as one of the best players in his position that year, a remarkable rise for a quarterback for whom very little was expected.

Talent

One of the great conundrums around career success, in whatever field, is the extent to which it is down to natural talent or other factors. In my experience, the secret to success is multi-faceted, a combination of talent, hard work, luck, judgment and environment. The right mindset also plays a vital role. Natural talent can provide an initial impetus, but it is never sufficient on its own to generate long-term success.

Significant consistent effort and dedication to learning and improving core skills can raise a lower level of natural talent and/or refine natural talent to reach its full potential. Luck, random events, and circumstances also have an impact, as can the opportunities and support available, such as education, resources, and mentorship. Often, the crucial difference is hard work and a growth mindset, the way in which an individual perceives and responds to challenges as opportunities to learn and grow.

For me, there was a foundational core of talent in terms of my numeracy and writing skills, passed on genetically from my parents, and nurtured in a loving and supportive home environment, then through school and university. I also had the good fortune to discover a pathway into the Forensic world, which both required and harnessed those skills, and refined them through experience and exposure to cases.

Opportunities to travel and broaden my experience also came along, but at every step on the journey, I had to put myself in a position to take them and be willing to move to take advantage of them. I also had to work really hard through school, university and professional exams, then many long hours, including a few all-nighters, to meet project deadlines at crucial times. I was willing to do it as it came with the role, but also because the work was meaningful, catching the bad guys, seeking truth, helping clients, and it aligned well with my values.

I could also see the positive impact I could have on the team. On one early leadership course, the national Forensic Partners and Directors all completed a psychometric assessment, which mapped work preferences to team roles, with a view to improving collaboration, coaching and leadership across the group. It was clear from this that my preference to be an *Explorer-Promoter*, a persuader, enjoying varied, exciting and stimulating work, was diametrically opposite to the preference of my boss to be a *Controller-Inspector*, valuing control, detail, standards and procedures, with a lower need for people contact.

At one level, that was an interesting dynamic for me to manage, but it also provided an avenue for me to make a difference with my strengths in an area of lower priority for my boss.

Indeed, my first six months in Manchester were something of a honeymoon period with the team, as my (relatively) fresh, open, and engaging approach appeared to be a welcome contrast to how things had been before. However, this was soon contrasted with the following six months, when the novelty had worn off and the team would hark back to how the Partner used to do things. It became apparent that people are neither as good nor as bad as they are perceived to be in any given moment.

After a year or so, things settled down and my style was generally accepted for what it was, as the team figured out when to come to me (for people, business development or practice management matters), or him (for particularly thorny technical issues).

I also figured out who my brains trust would be in the team, with different people playing key roles in helping me with team leadership, business development, managing engagements, and providing a barometer of team morale, with helpful counsel on when and how to intervene. I had never had an Executive Assistant before, and mine was invaluable in helping me navigate an increasingly busy set of responsibilities.

I particularly enjoyed working with a slightly older, technically excellent Senior Manager who possessed very good writing skills and was definitely capable of being a Director in his own right if he wanted to be. He didn't want to be a Director and preferred to have me in the senior role to take the flak or the flowers that came with responsibility. I really valued him and quickly came to rely on him as our complementary skills gelled well as a team: I would sell, front and have ultimate sign off; and he would deliver high-quality draft reports and manage and develop the junior members of the team. I was also the ideas man, and he was the barometer of whether they were any good - a "maybe" was all the confirmation I needed on the few occasions I came up with something creative that could actually work.

As the work rolled in, I was able to invest in building and growing a team of complementary talents, and I really enjoyed the team-building component of it. It was also underpinned by a great deal of hard work.

This was also true of Tom Brady, who, at the time, was building on his initial Super Bowl win on his journey to becoming the most successful player in NFL history, and his ultimate status as the 'GOAT', the Greatest of All Time. Given his success, he has some very clear views on the extent to which his undoubted talent propelled him to that success.

The crucial differences for him were his work ethic and his drive to succeed, as he says: *"To be successful at anything, the truth is you don't have to be special. You just have to be what most people aren't: consistent, determined and willing to work for it."*

In the ultra-competitive world of professional sports, talent alone was never going to be enough. As Brady says, *"Hard work beats talent when talent doesn't work hard"*.

I certainly couldn't rely on talent alone.

Almost Perfect

By 2007, Brady had won three Super Bowl titles, but it had been three years since his last one. That season, the New England Patriots embarked on one of the most successful seasons in NFL history, becoming the first team to complete a perfect 16-0 regular season on the way to setting multiple single-season records and reaching another Super Bowl. Brady was voted the NFL's Most Valuable Player once again. They were one final win from an historic perfect season, and huge 12-point favourites against the unfancied New York Giants in the Super Bowl.

Leading 14-10 with just over two minutes to go, one of the luckiest, most physics-defying catches ever changed the course of NFL history. Giants quarterback Eli Manning performed a Houdini style, last-gasp escape and threw the ball to David Tyree, who somehow managed to complete a catch by pinning the ball to his helmet under pressure on his way down (it's well worth a look on YouTube!). That miracle catch kept the Giants alive to score the winning points with 35 seconds to go and hand Brady the toughest loss of his career.

It was almost—but not quite—the perfect season. Indeed, it would be another seven years before Brady would win the Super Bowl again, a full decade-long gap between winning the big one.

By the middle of 2007, my life was almost perfect too. We welcomed our son, Cameron, into the world in June, and we were settling in nicely to life in Manchester. We had parents and siblings, family and friends come to visit, and we spent some lovely long weekends with Mark and Andrea, Lorna and Ewen, Chris and Jen, and Lynn and Gary, and their respective children. We had day trips to explore new locations like Dunham Massey and Tatton Park, and saw Kylie at Manchester Arena and Ronaldo at Old Trafford before the shutters came down and the realities of parenting started to take hold.

Drive

Brady subsequently explained how the Super Bowl loss to the Giants at the end of the 2007 season was pivotal to the drive and motivation he had to keep on playing and winning well into his 40s. He said, *"You wanna know which [Superbowl] ring is my favourite? The next one."*

He had a relentless drive and determination. He made it back to the Super Bowl four years later but lost to the Giants yet again, later reflecting: *"I think sometimes in life the biggest challenges end up being the best things that happen in your life."*

By late 2007, the first signs of significant challenges for the global economy were also on the horizon. One of the first signs of trouble was a run on Northern Rock, a significant UK bank based in Newcastle, in the North of England, with many customers queuing outside branches to withdraw their savings. Over a couple of days, an estimated £3 billion was withdrawn by customers, and the share price fell by 60%.

The bank had become heavily reliant on short-term wholesale funding to finance its ambitious growth in mortgage lending, and when global markets froze in the first credit crunch of 2007, it was unable to roll over its short-term debt, causing severe liquidity problems. The British Government and the Bank of

England ultimately had to step in and announce that they would guarantee all deposits held at Northern Rock. There would be more turbulence to come.

I felt I had settled in well in my first year at KPMG, and had worked on some interesting cases across different industries: a contract compliance review for a significant spin-off business in the utilities sector, which resulted in a multi-million-pound rebate; a fraud risk compliance review for a successful start-up comparison website; a consequential loss case worth millions in the motorhome sector; a fraud investigation for a University; and a fraud and corruption risk review across multiple business interests for a major conglomerate.

I could also see things that needed to change. For the first time in my career, I thought seriously about aiming for Partner, but more in recognition of the growth in the size of the team and the leadership and mentorship required for the team to reach its potential. I thought I had the capabilities to make a positive difference. If that was the case, did I have the requisite belief, drive, determination and willingness to do the work to make it happen? Could I let go of my imposter syndrome, the feeling that I wasn't capable of doing the job, which, in retrospect, had acted as a handbrake on the first decade of my career? And what would my unique selling proposition and personal brand be?

For the first time, I was beginning to have confidence I could do it. I now needed to have a conversation about what the firm required and what the timeframe would be. Little did I know that the impact of what would become known as the Global Financial Crisis would have on my ambitions and timelines, but that was just another challenge I would need to drive through.

Man In the Arena

In the ESPN series, *Man in the Arena*, Tom Brady provides a firsthand account of his record ten Super Bowl appearances and seven wins over three decades, as well as other pivotal moments in his career. He became the GOAT in his chosen sport through belief, consistency, dedication and determination, as the master of hard work and no excuses, and with a mindset and drive to be the best he could possibly be. As his career progressed, he underwent a physical transformation through education and commitment to a specific healthy living and wellness regime, involving diet, sleep and exercise, and since the end of his playing career, he has applied the same approach and mindset to his new professional pursuits.

My path was much more modest, but by the end of 2007, some important lessons had laid the foundation for me, the most critical of which was exorcising my imposter syndrome and believing that I could make a real and meaningful difference. I was beginning to define my purpose and my plan, and I could see that the forensic mindset, which had served me well on individual projects, could also help me achieve professional health, wealth and happiness. I would now have to become the quarterback of my career and put myself forward as the Man in the Arena.

CHAPTER 7

BLOWING THE WHISTLE

"It is time the nation woke up and realised that it's not the armed robbers or drug dealers who cause the most economic harm, it's the white-collar criminals living in the most expensive homes who have the most impressive resumes who harm us the most. They steal our pensions, bankrupt our companies, and destroy thousands of jobs, ruining countless lives"

Harry Markopolos, who discovered and blew the whistle on the biggest-ever Ponzi scheme

The Global Financial Crisis

In 2008, the world exploded in the grip of the Global Financial Crisis (GFC), the most severe global recession since the Great Depression of the 1930s.

The proximate causes had built up over decades of deregulation and the financial innovations from the 1980s onwards. A combination of excessive speculation on housing values by homeowners and financial institutions, exacerbated by predatory lending for ever-riskier sub-prime mortgages, including NINJA loans (No Income No Job or Assets), many of which were packaged and re-packaged as apparently safe AAA-rated mortgage-backed securities, took financial markets to new heights.

As equity withdrawals, refinancings and defaults in sub-prime loans began to flow through in 2007, the complex web of derivatives tied to these loans collapsed, triggering a stock market crash and a full-blown liquidity crisis, including a run on a number of major banks, and ultimately the bankruptcy of Lehman Brothers in 2008. A severe global recession, credit crunch, banker bailouts, and a crisis in the Eurozone that lasted for many years followed, as carnage on Wall Street flowed through to devastate Main Street, impacting almost every sector of the economy.

The Greatest Ponzi

One of the poster boys of the GFC became a little-known (beyond financial markets) financier by the name of Bernie Madoff. A one-time Chairman of the NASDAQ stock exchange, he had founded a stock brokerage business in the 1960s, which had become very successful, high-profile, and well-respected on Wall Street. He had also subsequently founded a low-profile, highly exclusive and secretive asset management investment business. It was through this part of the business, that he effectively masterminded the largest Ponzi scheme the world has ever seen, worth an estimated $64 billion over three decades by the time he was finally arrested in December 2008.

So, what is a Ponzi scheme?

Although similar schemes existed before him, the size and scale of the fraud perpetrated by Charles Ponzi made his name synonymous with the one-man con. In 1919, Ponzi launched a business based on arbitraging international reply coupons, a type of postal voucher, claiming that he could buy them cheaply in Europe and redeem them for more in the USA, promising investors a 50% return in 45 days. However, the logistics failed, so Ponzi had to start paying early investors with money from new ones. As his scheme ballooned rapidly, he pulled in millions of dollars before it ultimately collapsed by August of the following year.

A Ponzi scheme creates the illusion of a secretive investment strategy or exclusive opportunity, with returns appearing *'too good to be true,'* and/or suspiciously consistent, regardless of market conditions. It is centralised with the perpetrator of the scheme collecting funds and paying returns using funds provided by new investors, but there is no real product—just fake investment returns—and whilst victims believe that their money is invested, the reality is that the funds are simply shuffled around.

A Ponzi scheme is similar to a Pyramid scheme, with the crucial difference being that Pyramid schemes are crowd-sourced hustles relying on constant new recruitment and investment at the base of the pyramid, in a "business opportunity" to pay returns to those further up the pyramid. Both schemes rely on a constant flow of new participants, but eventually collapse when investors demand their money back or new recruitment slows.

The story of how Madoff got away with it for so long and at such scale is one of greed, narcissism, cunning, incompetence and regulatory failings on an epic scale.

Madoff's investors were typically wealthy individuals and establishment families from North America and Europe, but also included a significant number of individuals who trusted him with their entire retirement savings. As the investment fund established a track record of regular, consistent, above-market returns over many years, more funds were invested and new investors were attracted, but Madoff retained very close control of who could join and how much was disclosed.

It became apparent that Madoff never lost and always beat the market, often buying immediately before prices went up and selling immediately before prices went down, but when investors asked for details of this mercurial strategy, they were rebuffed and told they could sell if they wanted. Madoff's notoriously secretive and opaque operations and refusal to disclose details of investment strategies, deemed too complex for clients to understand, maintained control, discouraged scrutiny, and allowed the fraud to grow over time. Many investors were seduced by the illusion of exclusivity and steady above-market returns, making them hesitant to withdraw funds or ask too many questions.

Madoff's narcissism was also central to how he operated, as he carefully curated an image of competence and exclusivity that fed his need for admiration and respect. He could be charming and articulate, adroit in using financial jargon to impress investors and regulators, but he could also be cold and critical, bullying detractors and dismissing criticism. Perhaps his most narcissistic trait, which is often present in the psychology of fraudsters, was the extent of his emotional detachment, lack of empathy, and any genuine remorse for his victims, many thousands of whom lost fortunes as a result of his scheme.

The tragedy of Madoff's Ponzi scheme was that it was not especially complex, but it did require discipline from his team to create the paper trail of fictitious transactions for investors year after year. A potentially plausible series of false trades and printed statements, aged by coffee spills and crumpled paper, created a parallel universe of apparent returns for investors. Most would not cash out as the returns were so good (on paper), and there was always an influx of sufficient new investment funds to cover withdrawals when requested. In true Ponzi style, cash flow was king, and was always available to take from Peter to pay Paul.

Whilst the stock brokerage business operated from the 19th floor of a plush Manhattan office, the Ponzi scheme was operated from a much more basic 17th-floor workshop, with very limited access and almost zero visibility beyond Madoff and his core team. Whilst he and his team were cunning and controlled in how they manipulated and manufactured "evidence" of trades at key moments when major investors, hedge funds and regulators probed, the underlying logic could and should have raised the alarm.

In fact, as early as 1999, a Boston money manager, Harry Markopolos, did raise the alarm. A numbers savant and options trader, Markopolos was asked by his bosses to reverse engineer Madoff's trading results by duplicating his purported investment strategy, and concluded that it was impossible to do so, and that, in all likelihood, Madoff was running a Ponzi scheme. He took his findings to the SEC, but the regulator dismissed his concerns, preferring to believe in Madoff's reputation for investing prowess as a pillar of the Wall Street establishment. This pattern of activity was repeated consistently over the years, with Markopolos continuing to blow the whistle on Madoff to the SEC in 2000, 2001 and 2005, laying out a comprehensive case in a report entitled *"The World's Largest Hedge Fund is a Fraud."*

Still, the SEC's response was inadequate, ignoring multiple red flags, and missing numerous opportunities to launch a thorough investigation. And even when they did conduct examinations, these were conducted by inexperienced teams who were no match for Madoff and his team. In the end, a lack of scepticism, and an over-reliance on Madoff's reputation allowed the fraud to go on much longer and grow much larger than it ever should have done. Estimated to be around $7 billion in 2000, it had ballooned to $64 billion by the time the music stopped, an indictment of the responsible authorities. As Markopolos said, *"The government didn't do its job when the institutions needed to be held accountable. If you see something's wrong, you can't just turn the other way. The regulatory system was totally rotten from top to bottom."*

By late 2008, the world had fundamentally changed for both Madoff and Markopolos.

The GFC had created an avalanche of frightened investors heading for the exits and rushing to close out their investments, a tsunami event for Madoff, for which there was insufficient cash to go around. A desperate Madoff bowed to the inevitable, confessed to his family, and was arrested in December 2008.

Markopolos, on the other hand, inspired by his years as a financial sleuth investigating Madoff, retrained as a Certified Fraud Examiner, and embarked on a noble new career as a forensic investigator.

Keep Calm and Carry On

Change is ever-present, and the economic trials and tribulations of 2008 blew many people off course. In the face of such change, the old British wartime slogan to *'keep calm and carry on'* had renewed resonance in the public psyche as a maxim for coping. It was also fundamental to the forensic mindset I tried to maintain in the face of whatever came my way. I was determined to work with the facts, analyse the evidence, focus only on what was in my sphere of control, and not be blown off course.

By late 2008, the nature of the investigations I was undertaking had also changed. We looked at liquidity and capital requirements in a number of financial institutions, given the nature of the credit crunch around us. There was also a deeper look at mortgage fraud on applications in relation to exaggerated (on non-existent) income and asset statements, as well as lenders approving loans without completing proper verification and due diligence processes. Broader corporate and governance failings also came to light, including financial statement manipulation to meet target results or bonus thresholds, which did not reflect reality, and the old chestnut of expense claim frauds, which may previously have been missed, were much more apparent in suddenly tougher economic times.

KPMG's Fraud Barometer report around this time touched on the changing nature and value of reported fraud cases across the UK, with a sidebar to each region. I fronted the media in the North West. Over the next few years, I provided annual commentary on what trends were up, down, new and emerging, with a view to raising the profile of fraud risk to organisations in our area, to help manage risks and exposures, and to improve defences to prevent, detect and respond to issues as they emerged. Fraud risk frameworks, assessments, and controls were fundamental in managing internal and external fraud risks. As time went on, the importance of forensic technology, analytics, data mining, matching, and interrogation techniques, as well as cyber response capabilities, became increasingly important.

The perfect case to illustrate this was Lexi Holdings, run by mercurial local tycoon Shaid Luqman and his brother and fellow director. At its peak, Lexi Holdings had a £300m turnover and Luqman, the flamboyant boss of the business, lived in a luxury Cheshire mansion, travelled the globe in a private Gulfstream jet, and drove around in a luxury Bentley. He had also featured on the *Sunday Times Rich List*, and had been lauded as Young Entrepreneur of the Year. However, by the time we had been appointed, he and his brother had fled the country, and in an attempt to cover their tracks, virtually all accounting records we would typically want to investigate appeared to have been destroyed.

Apart from a single disk, which was recovered during the discovery process. From that disk, we were able to apply our forensic technology and investigative skills to reconstruct, from incomplete records and sensible working assumptions, a virtual audit trail of the key accounting records and transactions as an approximation of who did, and who knew, what, when and how. As a result, it was possible to demonstrate that, by falsifying entries in its loan books, the directors had effectively exaggerated how much the company was worth between 2000 and 2006, and had misled a syndicate of banks into lending significant funds, which were subsequently funnelled into secret family accounts in Pakistan, resulting in one of the largest frauds in UK banking history at that time.

When the case came to trial, Luqman and his brother were charged with conspiracy to defraud and conspiracy to falsely account. The Judge, David Stockdale QC, said: *"The fraud was complex and sophisticated and conducted on a massive scale – the ultimate purpose was to mask the diversion of large sums of money elsewhere for the benefit of the Luqman family."*

With echoes of Madoff, it also became clear that the banks were impressed by how Luqman presented as a sophisticated businessman, successful and hungry for greater success: *"What they saw was a man who was clever, articulate and personable, and who impressed them as a good person to do business."*

The banks did not know about the fraudulent mis-handling and failure of Luqman's previous business, or his previous criminal conviction for fraud, which could have been determined from our forensic intelligence checks. In the end, Luqman and his brother were sentenced in absentia to prison and disqualified as company directors.

It is a feature of forensic work that we are one of the true counter-cyclical businesses, as fraud and financial crime become more prominent during a recession, as do litigation and expert witness work (after a time lag), as contractual disputes increase, and companies have less to lose by having a crack at one another. As strains were felt throughout the economy, a couple of cases really touched the heartstrings.

I became an independent expert on a matrimonial case, acting on behalf of a wife whose husband moved on, leaving two young children, one of whom was disabled, and needed significant and expensive care. My role was to value the business, which the husband had (perhaps conveniently) concluded had been significantly adversely impacted by the GFC, was worth far less than before, and its future prospects were much less attractive. Disclosure was torturous and piecemeal, business commentary had taken a decisively negative turn (perhaps as a result of the GFC, but also perhaps conveniently coinciding with the timing of his departure), and cash flow pressure was significantly impacting the ability of the wife to maintain the family home, care for the children, and fund a long, drawn-out and expensive matrimonial case.

Good sense may have indicated that a settlement should be reached, but the case progressed all the way to trial, only for it to be settled on the steps of the court after much preparatory expense had already been incurred. At least a settlement had been reached. However, a few years later, the case took an unexpected turn when it was discovered, by chance, that the husband had been lying and had not disclosed all of his assets, as had been required by the court, including an undisclosed growth opportunity for the business, leading to the settlement being re-opened, a much higher valuation being supported, and a much more balanced and appropriate outcome obtained.

In another case, there was no good outcome to be achieved. It was another family case, but in this one, a brother was suing his father and his sister in relation to the value of shares in a family business, and the running of the company, following the death of the mother. It was one of the saddest cases I have ever been involved in, as the father was literally dying, having been told he had a matter of months to live. The case had been running for at least a couple of years by the time a final mediation had been called to try to resolve the matter.

It was hosted in our office, and I was on hand, having been involved in various share valuation aspects of the litigation. The emotion in the room was intense, and the father's health was visibly failing. The mediation was scheduled to run from 12 pm to 3 pm at the latest, with a view to reaching a settlement and avoiding having to go to trial. Lawyers, accountants, family protagonists, company officials and a mediator were all on hand, so it was an expensive exercise.

In the end, the mediation finally reached a settlement at almost 11 pm, with everyone (and particularly the father) exhausted. At least it was done. However, it subsequently transpired that one of the parties refused in the days after the apparent settlement to sign the deed, rendering the entire exercise a colossal and expensive waste of time and money.

Deep-set emotional grievances had won the day, and I felt very sorry for everyone involved in the family—they were a wealthy (although now less wealthy) family, but seemed deeply unhappy and riven apart, proving once again that financial wealth is absolutely no substitute for happiness.

As a postscript to 2008, our family had cause for real happiness as Sally became pregnant once again. Amidst the maelstrom of the GFC and the challenging economic environment, it was nice to be cocooned in our family environment and look forward to whatever 2009 had in store.

Bailouts and Bailiffs

The GFC is considered to be one of the five worst financial crises the world has ever seen, estimated to have resulted in losses of more than $2 trillion from the global economy. The long tail of economic woe from the Eurozone crisis, austerity measures, quantitative easing, and higher personal and Government debt arising from institutional bailouts, had a lasting impact deep into the following decades.

By 2009, whilst the Forensic business was doing well as the volume of counter-cyclical work increased to more than cover pricing pressures from the downturn, that wasn't the case across the firm. In the circumstances, the firm developed a novel approach to retaining talent and protecting jobs in a programme known as *Flexible Futures*.

The initiative encouraged staff to sign up to voluntary new terms and conditions, which included one of two options: reduce the working week by one day per week, or agree to take between 4 and 12 weeks leave at 30% pay. Given the scale of the downturn and the likely alternative of redundancies, this was generally accepted across the firm. I picked the first option, and it worked well given the forthcoming change in family dynamics.

In July 2009, our second baby was on the way. Indeed, after a false start, when we were sent home overnight from the hospital, the starter gun was fired, literally as soon as my head hit the pillow. Heather was on her way—and fast. Within moments, I was in the bathroom, on the phone to the emergency services, and effectively in the catch position as Heather was coming. She arrived in minutes.

Legend may be that I was a midwife to deliver my daughter, but the reality was that Sally did all of the work, without drugs, and I couldn't fail to catch. Sally was an absolute star. I didn't have time to think about it, and, even if I had, there wasn't exactly an opt-out. As it turns out, all emergency services calls in the UK are recorded, and we subsequently requested and received a copy of that call, so we have, in our possession, a recording of Heather's very first sounds. Once mother and baby were stable, I had the privilege of bringing through a 2-year-old Cameron, somewhat perplexed by the commotion, to meet his sister for the very first time.

On surveying the scene of devastation, a blood-soaked carpet, his mother slumped against the wardrobe, cradling this new "thing", he pronounced his verdict: *"Mummy made a mess,"* and was then almost instantly distracted by the excitement of the flashing lights of the ambulance, which had now arrived outside our window.

Over the next few hours, the house was abuzz with medics, both of Sally's parents, and a hive of activity. As Heather had decided to come early, I wasn't really at a clean edge at work, so having received all of the necessary approvals, given the selection of appropriate adults around the house, I was off to one last meeting before parental leave would begin in earnest.

Living off adrenaline, it was seen as quite the story to be up all night, deliver a baby, and still turn up to work. The team and client marvelled at my dedication, but the reality was that I was just glad to be out of the house, to sort out a few things at work, and begin my parental leave proper when all the fuss had died down.

Keep calm and carry on.

The next few weeks were a period of adjustment as we settled into life as a family of 4. Then one day, when I was still home, the doorbell rang. Sally answered, babe in arms, toddler at her feet. It was the bailiffs who presented us with an eviction notice, with a scheduled date of just over 2 weeks later. We were stunned!

We had sold our apartment in Edinburgh and were renting a part-furnished house in Manchester. Unbeknown to us, our landlady had fallen well behind with her mortgage payments, and racked up a series of debts. We had no idea, and, as it turned out, as tenants, we had no rights. The matter was between her and her creditors. Keep calm (ish) and carry on (but go visit and speak to her immediately).

She provided assurances that she would sort things out and enter into a payment plan to resolve the court action, but we had no evidence or way of ensuring that this would be enough. We needed a plan in case it wasn't. Fortunately, the crisis was averted, and the bailiffs never reappeared. However, the stress was difficult, and the potential for recurrence was never far away. We ultimately agreed to buy the house, including some of the furnishings, around nine months later, and now had control of our own destiny once again.

The Final Whistle

The final whistle was blown on the GFC when the developed economies of the world finally came out of recession in the second half of 2009. A more rational, sceptical, forensic mindset was back in vogue, given the failings of the banks and the regulators, as well as anger and pain arising from the bailouts.

Things were changing, and there was recognition that the market needed to be better and more consistently regulated. Given the downturn, my aspirations of making it to Partner were on hold, but we had grown as a family, and after two years of sudden credit crunch, crisis and change, my confidence was up, and I had learned, with experience, to keep calm and carry on.

CHAPTER 8

MANAGING MY LIFE

*"There are plenty of attributes that separate the great leader
from the good manager…. the great leader possesses an unusual
and essential characteristic – he will think and operate like an
owner, or a person who owns a substantial stake in the business"*

**Sir Alex Ferguson, former manager of Aberdeen and
Manchester United, author of *Managing My Life***

Northern Lights

Between 1980 and 1986, thanks to the leadership of (not yet Sir) Alex Ferguson, there was a viable alternative for football-mad Scottish schoolboys, beyond the traditional *Old Firm* powers of Rangers and Celtic. I was one of those schoolboys.

These were the glory days of Aberdeen Football Club, which included a haul of three Scottish league titles, four Scottish Cups, a European Super Cup, and a glorious night in Gothenburg in 1983, when the mighty Real Madrid were vanquished in the European Cup Winners' Cup final. To this day, it was the last time that Real Madrid were beaten in a European final (they have won all ten subsequent finals), and the last time a team outside Glasgow won a Scottish league title (Rangers and Celtic have won all 40 subsequent titles). The Northern Lights of Aberdeen sparkled with success, and the historic nature of those achievements have grown in the rear-view mirror.

In November 1986, when Manchester United called, it was inevitable that Ferguson would move on. The challenge of revitalising a moribund giant, which hadn't won an English league title in almost 20 years, and the prospect of knocking arch-rivals Liverpool off their perch, was impossible to resist. It took more than three turbulent years, but in 1990, he won the FA Cup, his first trophy at the club.

By the time I arrived in Manchester in 2007, his trophy haul at United had grown to an amazing eight Premiership titles, five FA Cups, two League Cups, a European Cup Winners Cup, a European Super Cup, an Intercontinental Cup and, famously, a European Champions League win in 1999, a total of 19 trophies in 17 years. I was very much a fan.

A working-class boy from Glasgow, of a similar vintage and background to Billy Connolly, they were born within a year of each other and within five miles of each other. His father also worked in the Glasgow shipyards. Ferguson had a respectable playing career as a centre forward, including two years at Rangers and four caps for Scotland, recording a healthy number of goals for both. However, it was in his managerial career that he really made his mark.

Known for his fiery nature, super-competitiveness, and will to win, his *'hairdryer treatment'*, the intensity and force of his reprimand was like being blasted by a hairdryer, became legendary. He also commanded huge loyalty, respect, and a deep connection with his players.

Now that I was in Manchester, I was intrigued to see his team under the lights of Old Trafford. Over my first three years in the city, United won three consecutive Premiership titles, a League Cup, another European Champions League, and their first FIFA Club World Cup. I had no particular loyalty to United, but it was great to see a world-class team, orchestrated by Ferguson, featuring the talents of Ronaldo, Rooney, Giggs, Scholes and Tevez, in their pomp and on my doorstep. It was an object lesson in leadership, team building, and peak performance, and also provided great entertainment.

Squeaky Bum Time

One of the great quotes attributed to Ferguson is his articulation of *"squeaky bum time,"* that tense, fraught, pressure-cooker environment of the final run-in to the league season, when focus has to be laser-sharp and performance at an absolute peak to win the title. Like Cathy Freeman in an Olympic final, or Tom Brady in a Super Bowl, it is about performing at your absolute best to achieve your objective.

As always, preparation is key, but performance is paramount. Not everyone can handle the pressure, but it was fascinating to hear how Ferguson did it in his autobiography, *Managing My Life*.

Over the course of 2010, I was preparing for that moment, having successfully navigated the nine months of the league campaign, known as the Partner development process, the final few matches of the two-day intensive Partner assessment centre, and was heading into the final day of the season with it all on the line in the Partner panel interview.

It was *'squeaky bum time'* and the next sixty minutes would be death or glory (or, less dramatically, pass or fail). I had a one-page ten-minute presentation and an open season Q&A on any topic the panel chose to cover. I spent a number of weeks preparing for my final, practising my pitch, running through mock panels, taking on feedback, and researching the business news to be as well appraised of the firm, business, financial and world news as possible.

My one-pager featured photos of two men: a jubilant Ferguson holding the European Champions League trophy; and me in my suit. Two Scots, who came to Manchester to unleash unprecedented success. Metaphor as masterstroke, the pitch obvious.

One was world famous and had achieved it all after 24 years in role, the other was a work in progress, but on track after 3 years in role. Always worth remembering that Ferguson had won nothing until year 4, but management invested in him and were handsomely rewarded by the success that followed. It was worth investing in making me a Partner, and the riches would follow.

Actually, it wasn't entirely successful, as I could have been asked if I had a temper, or was inclined to throw boots at players Beckham-style, or bring out the hairdryer treatment, but it was all done in a spirit of good humour, and the panel went well. To be fair, there was substance and depth to my business and personal case, my track record was strong, my financials were good, and the feedback from clients, staff and Partners was persuasive, so I was confident I could perform. The cake was good, but Fergie's icing topped it off beautifully.

The following day, I had a call to say, *"it's looking good for you….at the moment"*, which had me in two minds in one sentence, but a few days later, it was confirmed that I would be offered a partnership in the firm, effective 1 October 2010. I was delighted, and my squeaky bum could finally relax.

Listening and Loopholes

Becoming a Partner was one thing; *being* a Partner was something different entirely. I had achieved a certain status in the firm, the business world, and the community, but I was also now on the lowest rung of a completely different ladder. Interestingly, no one put any pressure on me to perform, to generate revenue or to grow the business, it was all intrinsic, self-generated, and borne from my own desire to justify the trust and faith the firm had placed in me. Joint and several liability with some 600 fellow UK Partners, most of whom I didn't know, also took a while to get my head around, not to mention the wider global firm of almost 8,000 Partners and 300,000 staff worldwide.

I was soon to be introduced to the wider firm at the Global New Partner Conference in Beijing. It was a fascinating three days in the capital of the world's emerging economic superpower, with excellent speakers on geopolitics, business, technology, economics and world affairs, with a cohort of new Partners from around the world, including cultural activities and events in Tiananmen Square, the Great Hall of the People, and a trip to the Great Wall of China. The culture was fascinating, the networking excellent, and the contacts made and developed there have lasted the test of time.

Indeed, the importance of establishing and growing networks from different cities, countries, sectors and specialisms, is an important skill for all professionals. Over coffee, lunches, drinks, meetings or seminars, an ability to be curious, establish connection, form relationships, and find mutual areas of relevance and interest become increasingly important in more senior roles. My home base may have been Manchester, but I was increasingly building my network in Leeds, Liverpool, London and internationally too.

As a Partner, my role was now part-owner and representative of the firm on a wider range of topics, my technical expertise and track record assumed, and my role was to grow the business, sales, client relationships and team, implying less time available to be *on the tools* of individual projects. I still had overall responsibility for projects, but had to be lighter touch and empower my team to play a larger role.

As Ferguson says: *"Distinguish between power and control, delegate, be decisive."* Some people struggle with the evolution of responsibilities, as the skills that make them successful in one role are different from the skills they need to succeed at the next level. The roles of Senior Manager, Director and Partner require a different balance of time and focus, and whilst delegation is key, overall responsibility remains, so getting the right balance of trust, but also verifying the quality of output, was important. I was energised by the change.

There was also a subtle change in the team, as I now took formal responsibility for Forensic in the North, as the Senior Partner built out our national Major Project Advisory practice. My team across Manchester, Leeds and Preston was now 30 strong (similar to Ferguson's first team squad at United), so I was now responsible for the hopes, dreams, aspirations and livelihoods of a much larger group of people. And the more people there are, the more people *issues* there are.

It was important to get the right balance of strategic direction, empowerment and engagement of hearts and minds, as well as truly understanding my team as individuals. Fortunately, I had an excellent leadership team, who all played their part in driving forward their areas of the business and development of our people.

I also learned from Ferguson, who had some fantastic lessons in leadership. He knew there were certain non-negotiables for everyone in the team, but he also understood that each player was an individual, and tailored his approach accordingly: Cantona was given freedom and trust, knowing he thrived on autonomy and the responsibility of being a role model for the younger players; Ronaldo was pushed to be the best, knowing he had the talent and ambition to get there, but also kept him grounded within the team; and a young Rooney had mentorship and tough love, particularly in the early years, to help him mature as a professional.

Ferguson also adapted to changing player attitudes over time, embracing sports science, and evolving his tactics to stay ahead of the curve as he built and re-built several successful Manchester United teams over the years. I learned a lot from seeing how he did it.

Ferguson highlighted the importance of listening in any team dynamic when he said: *"There's a reason that God gave us two ears, two eyes and one mouth. It's so you can listen and watch twice as much as you talk. Best of all, listening costs you nothing."*

It was sound advice, and taking the time to watch and listen led to much better outcomes and decisions, and helped create a platform for the team to grow.

In fact, it was one of Ferguson's misdemeanours that led to one of my more challenging learning experiences in my first year as a Partner. In 1999, Ferguson had been caught avoiding a traffic jam by driving down the hard shoulder of a motorway. His lawyer, Nick Freeman, who cultivated the nickname *Mr Loophole*, successfully argued that Ferguson had no choice due to a stomach bug, and he was rushing to the toilet at United's training ground. So began the legend of Mr Loophole, whose forensic knowledge of the UK Road Traffic Act helped him make millions in fees by defending celebrity clients such as David Beckham, Jeremy Clarkson, Andrew Flintoff and others, often highlighting technicalities, procedural errors, late notices, and mistaken identities, to force magistrates to throw the cases out.

In 2007, a key member of Mr Loophole's firm, was arrested, and subsequently alleged that this was a malicious prosecution, and that the reputational damage from his arrest had led to his departure from the firm, resulting in a significant consequential loss of earnings that he would otherwise have made 'but for' his arrest. This required an assessment of the earnings he would have made based on various factors, such as the number of clients, the expected fee arrangements, and the remuneration agreement with Freeman. The lawyers also argued that he was the key driver of success behind the scenes, as the primary liaison point with clients and barristers as soon as an issue arose.

The fact pattern was challenging as historic earnings in the 3 years before the arrest had been modest, then grown, then exceptional in the final year immediately before the arrest. In addition, the information available was necessarily incomplete and piecemeal. It was challenging to fully separate the extent to which Mr Loophole, the individual, and/or others, could have influenced what the future size of the business and its results could have been, including the extent to which there were true barriers to entry for other competitors coming into the market and taking market share, which may have had an adverse impact on pricing and earnings.

The key question was what the most reasonable expectation of earnings would have been, based on the information available at the time: would they have continued to grow exponentially into the future in each subsequent year, or were there other factors and uncertainties that an independent expert would reasonably be expected to take into account in determining the most likely future earning pattern?

There were certainly some passionate and definitive views to consider. I was the independent expert, hired by the lawyers but with an overriding duty to the court. I was absolutely committed to the integrity of my role, and my report to the court was balanced, reasonable and very much my opinion.

The case ultimately went all way to the High Court in London, and the paparazzi were there as I arrived to give evidence. They were not there to see me as Roman Abramovic and Boris Berezovsky were simultaneously battling it out in an adjacent courtroom, but the sense of drama was there all the same. I was in the witness box for a number of hours, and I was pleased that I had stuck to my guns and maintained my professional integrity and reputation. It was another object lesson to do the right thing, and I was glad to have come through the fire.

Trusting Talent

A signature theme of all Ferguson's teams, from his Dandy Dons of the early 80s, to the Class of '92, to the investments in Rooney and Ronaldo, was his keen eye for and trust in talent, irrespective of age. When he promoted youngsters like Beckham, Butt, Scholes and Neville from his Class of '92 in one go, commentator Alan Hansen famously said, *"you'll never win anything with kids."* Ferguson promptly proved him wrong by winning the league title.

It was a lesson I took to heart, and as I built out my team in Manchester, I was keen to ensure there was always opportunity for talent to shine, irrespective of years on the clock. There were some very smart and capable people coming through, and I was regularly impressed and never let down by any of them. Indeed, it was possible to tell from relatively early in their careers who the potential future Partners and Directors in the firm could be.

We worked on a number of disputes with local law firms such as Addleshaws and Eversheds, Pinsents and Pannone, DLA and DWF, and there were some great lawyers at all of these firms. A few memorable cases included:

- The consequential losses arising from product recall of health supplements and soft drinks from supermarket shelves, and the impact of short and long-term reputational damage on results;
- The critical path analysis of accountabilities for variations, delays and cost over-runs on construction contracts, which utilised the expertise of our excellent forensic quantity surveyors; and
- The quantification of material damage and business interruption from the compulsory purchase and relocation of business premises.

Case variety really was the spice of life, and the team was excellent.

One of my personal favourites was for a funeral care business, and allegations in a local newspaper that staff members had mistakenly disposed of human ashes, mixed with grit, which was then used on an icy driveway outside its premises. Putting aside the sensationalised reputational damage, this required an assessment of the loss of business, which had been incurred as a result of people choosing to take the funerals of loved ones, and their ashes, elsewhere. This required analysis of actual and expected death rates, adjusted by year, location and weather, and the drop in 'market share' of funerals in the immediate aftermath of the article.

Our investigations were equally exciting: an accountant sprucing results to obtain a higher bonus to pay off his gambling debts; a lawyer over-stating fees and leaving a trail of bad debts after his departure; a Manager running up significant personal expenses on his company credit card; even a Premiership footballer attempting to pay off his legal fees in cash in a brown paper bag to minimise the paper trail associated with the house he had purchased for his pregnant girlfriend so his wife wouldn't find out.

We were beginning to really gel, have fun and grow as a team - a hair-raising rally around the Ribble Valley one year, a law firm quiz night another, a few team celebratory events at other times, even a memorably adventurous late-night drive on a flat tyre in Switzerland on the way to a client. There was also more connection beginning to happen nationally, through projects and conferences, and I became more integrated with the national Forensic Partners.

As our business grew, so did our business development, hosting fun client events, such as Polo in Chester, football in Liverpool, Strictly Come Dancing in Manchester, even a Take That reunion concert (featuring Robbie). It was a great team and a great time.

We are the Champions

Sir Alex Ferguson's first trophy as a Manager opened the floodgates to one of the most successful periods in the history of English football. His key attributes as a leader included discipline, focus, confidence, resilience, adaptability, a winning mindset, and an ability to constantly build for the future.

As I reflected on my first couple of years as a Partner, I was increasingly doing all of those things. I was exactly where I wanted to be, doing meaningful work, being authentic to myself and acting with integrity, as my mindset transitioned to leadership and being an owner of the business.

In April 2013, I was at Old Trafford to see Robin van Persie score a stunning hat-trick as Manchester United were crowned Premiership champions for the 13th and last time in Ferguson's reign as Manager. It was a special celebration, particularly as he announced his retirement just two weeks later.

Manchester United have not won a league title since.

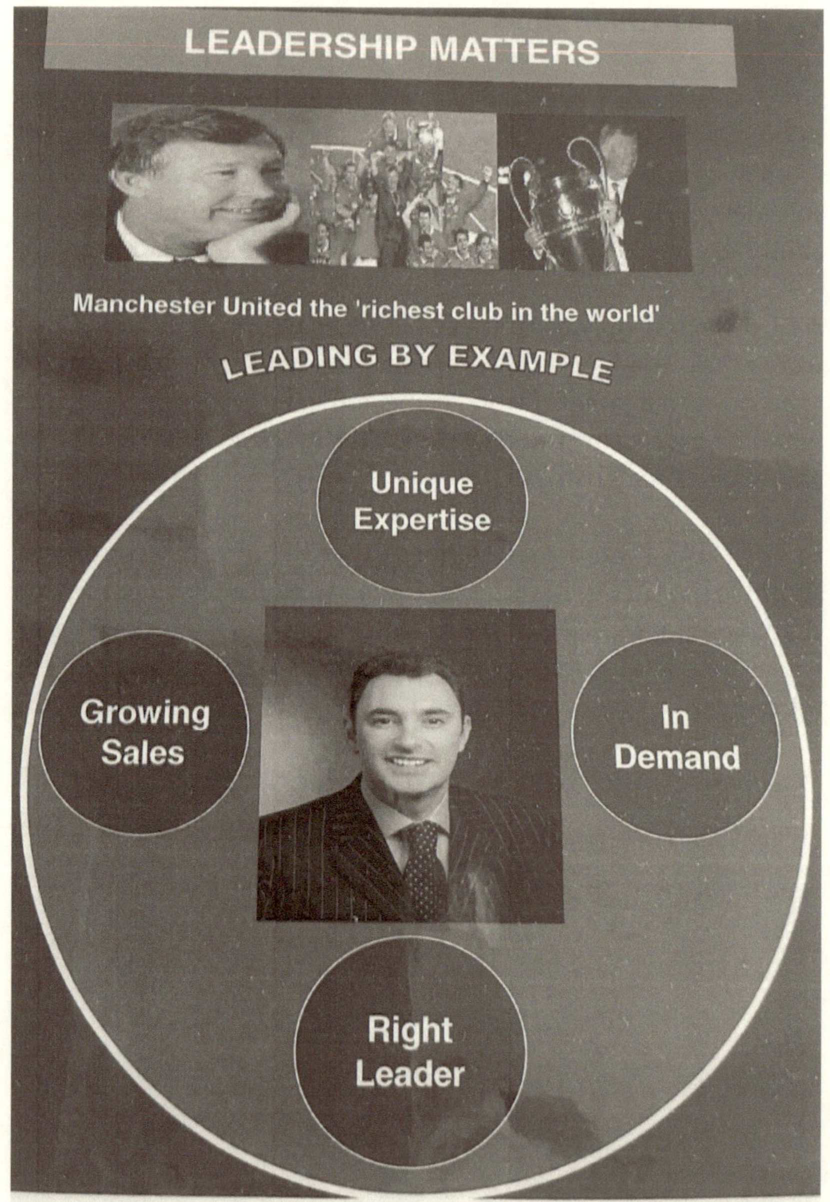

Learning to lead by example, my partnership pitch, 2010

"Supply Chain Expert" Martin Dougall (cunningly
disguised in attractive hairnet), with BBC Breakfast
TV News correspondent Steph McGovern
on-site at a glamourous pie factory in Wigan, 2014

CHAPTER 9

CATCH ME IF YOU CAN

"Technology breeds crime, and we are constantly trying to develop technology to stay one step ahead of the person trying to use it negatively"

Frank Abagnale, con artist turned security consultant, immortalised in the movie *Catch Me If You Can*

Cat and Mouse

The Stephen Spielberg movie *Catch Me If You Can* tells the story of infamous teenage con man Frank Abagnale, played by Leonardo DiCaprio, and the cat and mouse showdown he has over his teenage years with dogged FBI investigator, Carl Hanratty, played by Tom Hanks. Abagnale goes on a wild ride impersonating a Pan Am pilot, a doctor in Georgia, and a lawyer in Louisiana, all before the age of 21, when he is finally arrested and charged with auto larceny, theft, forgery and fraud.

Whilst a number of these stories have subsequently been debunked or disputed, the spectre of the charming con man continues to hold sway in the public imagination, and the existence of fraudsters, swindlers and conmen are all too prevalent in our daily news.

By 2013, I had become well-versed as the spokesman for the KPMG Fraud Barometer in the North of England. With the nature, timing, and amount of fraud and financial crime increasing year on year, the profile of a fraudster was constantly evolving with developments in technology.

Some of the high-profile cases recorded in the region included: a gang setting up 23 bogus construction firms to steal £4m in a VAT fraud; three men jailed over a recycling scam, stealing more than 90,000 plastic bread trays from a national bakery, worth £500,000; a student found guilty of conning 6 women out of £186,000 as part of a 'lonely hearts' scam; and an investment banker who stole more than half a million pounds from wealthy clients. Fraud is always innovative and exploitative, and the use of technology was increasingly sophisticated.

We also produced our Profile of a Fraudster survey around this time, providing insights into the typical attributes and motivations of fraudsters, the environments in which they flourish, the evolution of global fraud trends, and the innovative use of technology. The typical fraudster was male, in middle to senior management, trusted within the organisation, and had been there a long-time - high trust plus high opportunity plus low suspicion meant high risk. Insider fraud threat was prevalent, with businesses hit hard by unscrupulous management exploiting senior roles to engage in illegal activities.

The interplay between fraudsters and forensic investigators, like Abagnale and Hanratty, is very much a game of cat and mouse, with each new innovation developed by the fraudster having to be followed, found and shut down by the investigator.

Come Fly with Me

The song "Come Fly with Me" is featured in *Catch Me If You Can* as it charts Abagnale's journey impersonating a Pan Am pilot, having charmed and scammed his way to obtain an airline ID card, pilot's licence and uniform, finding his way onto several Pan Am planes, allegedly flying some two million miles over the period of his fraud.

I found myself flying for more legitimate reasons, having taken on a role in our Global Dispute Advisory Partner group. KPMG was a key sponsor of the Global International Bar Association (IBA) conference, attracting over 5,000 lawyers, judges, barristers and legal professionals from over 100 countries each year.

As lawyers were key clients for dispute advisory and investigation engagements, it was a valuable conference to attend. It also didn't harm that the venue changed each year, and over time, I made it to Dublin, Boston, Tokyo, Vienna and Washington DC, building some great relationships with clients and colleagues from around the world, attending some fascinating seminars and events in amazing venues, all in the name of business development. I thoroughly enjoyed it.

I was also asked to take on other leadership roles as a Partner.

I joined the Manchester Board alongside Partners leading our Audit, Tax, Transactions and Consulting teams, which provided invaluable insights into the local market, challenges, business development initiatives, and work in the community. I found that the more I contributed, the higher the return, as insights on how the firm was helping other clients and teams sparked more ideas and opportunities for me to bring our niche Forensic offerings to a wider audience. It was through these links that regular speaking slots at Accounting update seminars, sector dinners, and client service team meetings came through, which became a virtuous circle, further increasing our profile and flow of work for the team.

I was also asked to join our national Risk Consulting (RC) leadership team, with responsibility for Forensic and RC in the Regions (i.e. everything outside London). This sounds grander than it was, as the financial geography of the UK means that specialist expertise often gravitates to London, where the larger clients and projects need that expertise. As a result, almost 75% of Forensic and RC teams were concentrated in London. The reality of the UK's transport geography, ironically, meant that London was also the most convenient place for regional leaders from the North, South, Midlands, and Scotland to meet.

Nevertheless, the challenges of scale and commuting apart, there were some excellent pockets of capability, clients and projects done by around 200 or so actuaries, accountants, technology risk, cyber, financial risk and forensic professionals in our offices outside London. The role also gave me early insight into being part of running of a £300 million national RC business.

Finally, I also took on a national role leading our Power & Utilities sector for RC. I had previously worked on forensic projects with Electricity North West, Northern Grid Networks, and ScottishPower. On the basis that a little knowledge is a dangerous thing, I threw myself into learning more about the sector, attending internal sector meetings and external conferences.

There were parallels to what had been happening in post-GFC financial services, with rising risk and regulatory expectations: ensuring compliance; avoiding mis-selling; treating customers fairly (particularly vulnerable customers); consumer protection; and promoting consumer choice to switch providers. It was also fascinating to be in a new world of carbon pricing and critical infrastructure, decarbonisation and digitisation, renewables and resilience, and waste management and water quality. I was enjoying being able to branch out from core forensic work to adjacent areas, working alongside risk and regulation professionals nationally.

Some interesting projects flowed with many of the Big Six energy companies, such as Centrica and Eon, Npower and EDF, as well as Drax, Sellafield and UK Power Networks. One of my favourites was for the energy regulator, Ofgem, to review and recommend improvements to its enforcement regime, to become *Faster, Higher, Stronger*, very much in vogue as the motto of the 2012 London Olympics, which was also taking place around that time.

The goals were to: improve the effectiveness, transparency, and strategic alignment of its investigation framework; assess and improve enforcement policies and procedures; ensure investigations created a credible deterrent to non-compliance; and respond to the increasing complexity and volume of contested cases. This was a perfect blend of my forensic experience and burgeoning sector knowledge, and made a meaningful difference in the sector.

A couple of years later, Ofgem's CEO joined KPMG as a Partner, and we had another opportunity to work together on a number of projects designed to uplift quality in the sector.

By 2013, I was balancing multiple roles across the country and thoroughly enjoying it. I had also discovered the secret to doing so was like a Matryoshka, the series of progressively smaller Russian nesting dolls, all contained within each other. I could make it work if all the roles I took on were effectively a subset of the central role of building a successful business. The firm had also invested in me, flying me to leadership development conferences in Istanbul, Barcelona and Frankfurt, as well as my first global Forensic conference in Zurich.

I was flying high.

You Really Got Me

The song "You Really Got Me" appears in *Catch Me If You Can* as the net begins to close in on Abagnale. In the movie, Hanratty first notices the pattern of forged Pan Am cheques using similar techniques, deducing that they are the work of a single individual. He begins tracking him across multiple states and concludes that the forger is impersonating a Pan Am pilot, giving him access to free flights and helping him evade detection.

When Hanratty almost catches him at a hotel, Abagnale pretends to be Secret Service Agent Barry Allen, whom he later discovers to be a comic book character, indicating his youth. Another clue to his background comes when Abagnale references the Yankees on a call. Hanratty's detective work, attention to detail, and piecing the clues together eventually lead him to Abagnale, a missing juvenile from New York state, whom he comes across in a picture in his yearbook at his mother's house.

Forensic attention to detail and persistence was also true of a number of investigations I worked on in my first few years as Partner, which included: theft of confidential information by an employee leaving a business and setting up as a competitor; a series of procurement fraud cases, sometimes involving collusion with suppliers, but often simply over-charging and false invoicing for services not provided; and false or inflated expense claims or insurance claims.

In almost every case, the fraudster had a back story that aligned with everything we had seen in the fraud triangle and the profile of a fraudster. A few were sophisticated, most were not, but it was always important to demonstrate and document the investigation process, the chain of evidence, being precise with everything, and setting out each aspect of the nature, timing and amount of the fraud.

The extent of attention to detail was different for everyone and some Partners were tighter than others. I came across one case where there were over 1,000 review comments on a draft report, and another occasion where the Red/Amber/Green traffic light reporting was amended to include two shades of Amber.

As my roles increasingly drew me to London, I tried to involve my local team on larger London projects. Interesting ones included being an expert on a contentious divorce case, working with a formidable London law firm, Sears Tooth, whose main protagonist was known as "Jaws," given his reputation for tenacious advocacy, having worked on cases for the wives of celebrities such as Jude Law, Colin Montgomerie, and Roman Abramovich.

In another one, I acted as a single joint expert and arbitrator on a complex case for the British Museum. I also worked on a substantial case involving the multi-millionaire entrepreneur and activist investor, Robert Tchenguiz, whose business interests had once included M&B, Sainsbury's, and SCi Entertainment, which ultimately led to giving evidence in the Royal Court of Guernsey.

At the same time, more local cases included a fascinating forerunner of Manchester City's Financial Fair Play dispute with UEFA, involving the accounting policies applied for depreciation and amortisation of player contracts, and the accounting treatment and disclosures of potential related party transactions.

There were also interesting compulsory purchase order cases from the acquisition and relocation of businesses from retail stores to supermarkets. And finally, there were quantum disputes arising from contaminated hummus removed from supermarkets, the integrity of the source ingredients in dog food and, most famously, the risks of horsemeat in lasagne.

The last one led to my debut appearance on BBC One Breakfast News. However, visions of stardom on the sofa with Susanna Reid were quickly dashed, as the brief involved a somewhat less glamorous detour to a pie factory in Wigan, and the issue of wearing regulation wellies, a white coat, and a hairnet. I looked fabulous.

The horsemeat scandal raged through the British winter of 2013, and as my team had done some exploratory work around investigating the integrity of the source of ingredients, as well as quantifying the impact of breach of contract when things go wrong, we were ideally placed to comment. I was armed with facts, figures and phenomenal phrases which, as any politician will know, were going to be shoehorned into my answers no matter how tenuously relevant they were to the questions.

My command of the detail around the *"457 stages in the journey from the farm to the fork"* may have lacked depth, but it definitely worked as a soundbite imputing great wisdom, as *"KPMG Supply Chain Expert Martin Dougall"* was emblazoned across the TV screen. I was whisked from TV to radio interview to BBC World News, and as my stardom stretched from Wigan to the world, I came back down to earth when I made it back to the office, as the 'hairnet hero' was on full display on a life-size poster defacing the walls around me.

Ah, the price of fame….

Media work continued the following year as BBC Breakfast asked for another appearance, and this time I made it to the studio. On this occasion, I was *"KPMG Economics Expert Martin Dougall,"* although I'm pretty sure their due diligence didn't stretch back to my last official thought about Economics, on completing my degree in 1993. That said, I must have acquitted myself reasonably well as none of the two million or so viewers complained about my commentary on the impact of the latest economic indicators on unemployment, inflation and wages. I was beginning to feel like an Abagnale-style imposter, but at least this time it was good enough to be wearing regular clothes in front of the nation.

Poacher Turned Gamekeeper?

Abagnale claims that he was a conman specialising in impersonation, forgery, and cheque fraud, and that after his arrest and conviction, he used his insights to help the FBI as an expert on fraud prevention.

Whilst true that Abagnale has been a security consultant over the past few decades, a lot of the detail in the movie *Catch Me If You Can* is embellished or made up, much like the real-life cons of the main protagonist. The true scale and success of Abagnale's activities is a pale reflection of what is portrayed in the movie, and he appears to have been largely unsuccessful as a petty criminal, being arrested and imprisoned on several occasions.

However, Abagnale still claims to be one of the world's most respected authorities on cybercrime, identity theft, scams, and forgery. Meanwhile, the character of Hanratty is loosely based on real-life FBI Special Agent Joseph Shea, who reportedly did not maintain contact with Abagnale after his arrest, and never publicly stated that Abagnale had worked for the FBI.

We didn't conduct any work for the FBI, but we were certainly involved in several proactive prevention and detection engagements. These were designed to protect our clients, improve controls, ensure compliance, and prevent issues arising in the first place.

In particular, we built tailored fraud risk frameworks, and anti-bribery and corruption risk assessments and protocols to comply with the US Foreign & Corrupt Practices Act, and the new UK Bribery Act from 2013 onwards. We also deployed forensic intelligence tools to support pre-employment screening, background checks and adverse press monitoring; to provide factual integrity due diligence in relation to corporates and individuals our clients were potentially getting into business with.

On a number of occasions, this led to termination of an agreement or decision not to go ahead, most notably putting a stop to a proposed multi-million-dollar investment in a factory in China, when it was determined that the extensive use of unpaid prison labour, discovered during the course of our review, was incompatible with company values.

Leaving On a Jet Plane

The song "Leaving on a Jet Plane" captures the poignant moment in *Catch Me If You Can* when Abagnale is extradited back to the USA from France.

Unlike Abagnale, I wasn't being extradited, but as we approached the end of 2014, it was definitely time for us to seriously explore a move back to Australia.

One of the commitments we made on moving back to the UK from Sydney in 2002 was to apply for Permanent Residency (PR) in Australia, and we were open with our parents and friends about this. There is a points-based system with points awarded based on: age (diminishing as you get older); educational qualifications; skilled employment experience; relevant occupations; English language proficiency; and prior work experience in Australia. We had sufficient points, and we thought we would go back to live in Australia one day.

In UK summers, we didn't give it much thought, but in UK winters, it was definitely a comfort to have Australian residency - our ticket to the sun - as an insurance policy, This was especially true in the first week of January each year when the TV show, *Wanted Down Under*, came on, charting the experience of UK families having an all-expenses trial week in Australia – it was almost cruel to put this on in the depths of winter, as people trudged back to work after the holidays.

We had obtained our PR in 2006 and, with some difficulty, were able to renew it in 2011. However, we now faced having to make a definitive decision before it expired for good in May 2016. Cameron would be 8 and Heather would be 6 in 2015, so we had navigated the early years, and whilst friendships had formed, they were not so deeply formed as they would later be as teenagers. I was also spending an increasing amount of time in London, and there was a reasonable prospect of potentially having to relocate at some point in order to continue progressing my career, which no one else in the family was thrilled about.

I had met the Partner who ran our Australian Forensic practice at a Global conference in Zurich, so at least it wasn't a cold call in the first instance. After a few discussions, it turned out that there were currently no Forensic Partners in Melbourne, and a number of those in Sydney and Brisbane were heading towards retirement over the next few years.

After further discussions with the Heads of Risk Consulting and Advisory, I was invited to spend a week in Sydney and Melbourne to explore further, undertaking some interviews and assessments on-site, which were duly arranged for March 2015. Those went well and, after a few months building the business and personal case and working through the details of the offer, whilst simultaneously working through the logistics of trying to pack up a house, a life, and a family, the contract came through and the deal was done - we were going back down under.

In the midst of all this, there were two huge projects to leave the UK with a big finish.

In January 2015, we were approached by a company that had discovered a significant unexplained black hole in its accounts, and was in urgent need of a forensic investigation. What started as small acorns, became the largest engagement I had ever led, with an army of forensic investigators, accountants and technology specialists camped on-site in Milton Keynes, first unravelling, and then helping to reconstruct, a more accurate picture of the financial statements over a multi-year period.

In October 2015, in my penultimate week in the UK, I was called to give evidence in one of the most sensational cases I had ever investigated. I had initially been asked to conduct a small investigation over a few days the previous year, under the guise of an 'internal audit', into some discrepancies in results, for a law firm at its overseas office in Brussels.

At the end of the process, I had discovered a significant fraud perpetrated by the Managing Partner of that office, which included:

- Misappropriation of funds for his personal benefit;
- Billing personal expenses, such as travel and accommodation for him and his family, including the services of a personal chef, on extravagant family holidays to the Carribean;
- Dishonest conduct, including charging personal expenses to the firm and then on to clients, and allocating those expenses to client matters without authorisation; and
- Charging certain clients for personal expenses as disbursements on client invoices.

It was one thing to defraud the law firm, but another thing entirely to pass on those costs to clients, and the reputational damage to the law firm from having to explain the situation and reimburse clients for those inappropriate charges was particularly damaging.

The initial investigation did not identify many issues. However, a review of credit card charges and travel costs revealed a process by which significant personal expenses were being bypassed in the expense claim process. I was then able to follow these expenses to their ultimate destination on client invoices. Interviewing staff members on the process and accounting for transactions also proved decisive, particularly one individual who requested a follow-up meeting outside the office, after working hours, to take me through the true accounting process and expensing of invoices, which had not been recorded in the accounts. Whistleblower input was brave and invaluable, and closed some vital gaps in the evidence.

However, the biggest challenge was the General Manager who shadowed me everywhere, and was clearly trying to provide cover for the Managing Partner, and had explanations for everything. She was so focused on distracting me, she insisted on taking me out for early meals and drinks every evening I was there. As I politely declined, and it became increasingly apparent that I was on the trail, her demeanour changed, and by the end of the investigation, she had also provided some damning evidence, which bolstered the case even further.

The Solicitors Regulatory Authority Disciplinary Tribunal ultimately found that the former Managing Partner's conduct was deliberate and dishonest, that he knew his actions were wrong but proceeded regardless, and that his behaviour was such that it would be undesirable for him to be involved in a legal practice going forward.

After some 500 projects in almost nine wonderful years in Manchester, it was time to hand over the reins. It was our time to be *'wanted down under'* once again, so whilst Abagnale's jet plane took him to prison, ours was bound for Melbourne....

CHAPTER 10

A LITTLE HELP FROM MY FRIENDS

"Here lies one who knew how to get around him men who were cleverer than himself"

Andrew Carnegie, 19th-century Scottish-American industrialist, multi-millionaire and philanthropist

Sweet Little Mystery

In 1987, the Scottish band Wet Wet Wet reached number five in the UK charts with one of my favourite songs, "Sweet Little Mystery," which may well have inspired my lifelong passion for the world of mysteries, intrigue, and puzzles. The following year, they hit the top with their first UK number one single, a cover of The Beatles' classic "With A Little Help from My Friends."

I have always loved music, as those around the office will know from the various ringtones I have imposed on them, but what really struck a chord was the core human need for connection, camaraderie, team spirit, and the ability to rely on your friends.

As I joined a new team in Australia, I wanted to be part of a team that would really bond and achieve something special together, a combination of mysteries and mateship. You may even spot some familiar song titles throughout this chapter.

A century earlier, another Scottish emigre, Andrew Carnegie, was present at the opening of the iconic Carnegie Music Hall, which he funded and dedicated as a gift to the city in which he made his fortune. From humble beginnings in Dunfermline, he moved to the USA at the age of 12, eventually making his fortune through his investments in railroads and steel, founding Carnegie Steel Company, which he ultimately sold for over $300 million in 1901.

Carnegie, too, believed in the power of teams, surrounding himself with talented and intelligent individuals, convinced that true success came from recognising his own limitations and enlisting the help of others. Carnegie also believed that wealth should be used to improve society, funding the creation of almost 3,000 libraries worldwide, inspired by his own self-education through borrowed books, founding Carnegie Mellon University, Carnegie Hall, and numerous trusts and foundations focused on education, peace, and science.

As a philanthropist, he encouraged the rich to give back, championing progressive taxation, and giving away US$350 million in his lifetime, almost 90% of his fortune, amounting to several billion dollars in today's money.

I was unlikely to be a trailblazer quite like Carnegie, but when I arrived in Melbourne, I saw some humble beginnings from which to build a successful team. The Forensic team included 9 in Melbourne within a total of around 50 nationally, and it soon became apparent that what had made the practice successful historically was ripe for refresh and renewal to be successful in future.

In my first 18 months, I led a *Forensic 2020* initiative to ascertain the views of leaders across our national team in relation to the political, economic, legal, regulatory, and technological changes that would likely impact the future strategic direction of our business. It was important for me to seek the best thoughts and ideas from our team, build relationships with emerging leaders, and co-design the future strategy of the business. This was particularly important given the imminent retirements of three of the four other Partners in the business in the next couple of years.

It was also important to get to know the Partners in Melbourne. Similar to my experience in Manchester, I had arrived in a new city where I knew (virtually) no one, but any anxiety I felt in putting myself out there was countered by my experience of having done it before, and I relished the opportunity to reinvent myself once again.

After a whirlwind 3 weeks of pre-Christmas introductory coffees, lunches and dinners, and saying yes to every invitation, the office shut down for the traditional festive/summer break when the whole Australian business world is on holiday. I came back in 2016 refreshed and raring to go.

In Melbourne, there were 3 strong technical Directors and a capable but timid team, some of whom lacked confidence. It was important to establish a new way of thinking and a place for everyone to thrive, so cultural change was necessary. In my experience, a critical environment is futile as it makes people defensive, wounds pride, creates feelings of resentment, and limits space to take risks for fear of failure, and a further doom loop of criticism. People wither under criticism but blossom when encouraged.

I remember asking someone on a senior promotion track to envisage themselves at their promotion celebration drinks and looking around the room as to who would be delighted they had made it – the very long pause and eventual single name response was telling. Any leader, at whatever level, in whatever industry, needs to create conditions that support, empower, and encourage their team with confidence to succeed, which will lead to them being invested in the success of their leaders. I set about trying to embed that culture throughout our team.

We quickly established team spirit through the tradition of 'Dougall's Donuts' on a Monday, team drinks on a Friday, and an open-door policy for ideas and initiatives to flow throughout the week. The *Forensic 2020* vision was coming together, and the work began to flow in.

One of my first engagements was an investigation into a registered training provider in vocational education, arising from allegations of false and misleading conduct in the marketing and selling of certain courses. This was a complex, high-volume and data-intensive exercise requiring significant input from junior staff and came at just the right time to allow me to push through plans to bring on 2 new graduates, and to work with 2 smart, capable, but previously marginalised staff.

A few early runs on the board also provided the confidence to bring in one of my former team members from Manchester on secondment, and a new Senior Consultant who was keen to relocate from Canberra. As the team evolved and Directors moved on, the foundations for a new, young, smart, capable team was emerging, built on youth, talent and opportunity. Inspired by Sir Alex Ferguson, I was building my own *Class of '92*.

We Could Be Heroes

In July 2017, I formally took on the role of Partner-in-Charge of Forensic in Australia. The *Forensic 2020* strategy was revealed with our Forensic Flower at its core. On the basis of keep it simple, make it memorable, this was a visual representation of six interlinked petals summarising the core elements of what we do with the word Forensic in the centre: Disputes; Investigations, Advisory; Financial Crime; Forensic Technology; and Forensic Analytics.

Our Forensic team was clearly still 4th of the Big 4 in Australia, and smaller than a number of our boutique competitors, but at least we had a strategy and a plan, and if we could keep the lights on through a year of transition, we would have a foundation to grow.

I knew we needed more experienced senior leaders in the team. As the clock ticked down on Partner retirements, and our current crop of Directors were still in development, with support of the firm, I scoured the market for the best Partner talent available.

Like a football manager approaching the transfer window with money to burn and holes to fill, I flirted with many, fled from some, failed with others and finally found the right crop for our team. By early 2018, the Forensic Fab Four were ready to join, consisting of two Partner hires from EY, a returning Partner from Deloitte, and a new Partner from industry.

My first challenge was setting the conditions for successful integration, including roles and responsibilities, to maximise the new Partner talent and energy coming in, while balancing the loss of experience, relationships, and ways of working resulting from three Partner retirements. I also had to navigate Director and broader team aspirations, which some perceived to have been dented by the new arrivals, ensuring there were still opportunities for everyone, making a substantive contribution to a bigger, better business.

Clarity on the internal promotion pipeline was crucial, following our big splash in the market, to ensure we continued to create and support pathways for talented people coming through. Understanding individual strengths, interests, and capabilities was also important, and, with a few exceptions, we had a sensible, structured matrix of service, sector, office and practice leadership responsibilities by the time we kicked off the new financial year on 1 July 2018.

I was energised by the buzz of leading a business, recruiting and shaping a (potentially) successful team, and winning hearts and minds to what we were aiming to achieve. I was also enjoying doing what Carnegie did – surrounding myself with smart people, all of whom were empowered to make a difference in their areas of responsibility.

Carnegie was right that *"no man will make a great leader who wants to do it all himself or to get all the credit for doing it"* and *"the secret of success lies not in doing your own work, but in recognising the right person to do it."*

Sometimes, a little humility and recognising what is important to other people is the key to success. I love the lesson from the story where Carnegie decides to name his new steel plant, the *'Edgar Thomson Steel Works'*, rather than the Carnegie Steel Works. Edgar Thomson was the President of the Pennsylvania Railroad, and I can only imagine which company the Pennsylvania Railroad then decided to buy the majority of its steel from.

Another famous Carnegie, the author Dale Carnegie, who wrote *How to Win Friends and Influence People*, reckoned that 15% of success was due to technical knowledge, and 85% was due to skill in social engineering—to personality and the ability to lead people. This is often confronting for people in highly technical roles, given the time and energy they devote to learning and honing their technical skills.

However, leading people and understanding how to inspire and motivate are skills that can be learned and honed with practice, much like any other skill. One of Dale Carnegie's core ideas was that the only way to get anyone to do anything was by making the other person want to do it, and to feel important doing it. Developing my leadership skills and understanding how to influence people was key to winning hearts and minds.

In 2018, we held our first national Forensic conference in years. The aspirational theme tune, "We Could Be Heroes" by Alessio, really set the tone for how we were coming together as a team.

Held over a couple of days, it was a combination of strategy, external speakers on future trends, technical training, a Forensic Fair to upskill everyone on the range of capabilities in our team, and lots of connection through team building events from Human Table Football to trivia quizzes, and fancy dress to Forensic team drinks, the climax of which was a live Scottish Ceilidh band to get everyone up and having a good time.

This was the launch of the good times, and we were on our way.

Money, Money, Money

I was enjoying working on the business rather than in the business, but I also felt a personal drive to lead from the front, and be credible and successful in the market. I still loved the intellectual challenge of forensic engagements and working with the team, and there were a couple of expert witness cases, which went all the way to court with substantial sums of money at stake. ABBA would be interested.

I was hired as an accounting expert in a bitter legal dispute between a founder and majority shareholder in a well-known restaurant chain, with his former business partner and ongoing minority shareholder. The minority shareholder claimed to have been denied access to company books and records, a breach of director and fiduciary duties, and manipulation, which he alleged was designed to devalue his stake in the business. The majority shareholder sought to drive a sale of the minority interest on the basis that the relationship had been irreparably damaged. My role was to consider the quantum in dispute, based on the value of the company, which was assessed at over $300 million at the time, and the impact on the value of the minority shareholding. As both parties appeared entrenched in their positions, this went all the way to the Federal Court of Australia and another appearance in the witness box for me.

My expert witness career expanded interstate when I was called to the Supreme Court of Queensland to give evidence in a multi-million-dollar claim for losses exceeding $60 million, arising from alleged breaches of contract and negligence in the marketing of sugar production. Estimated production volumes had been wrecked by severe weather, and the producer alleged that the contractor should have made better decisions to mitigate the financial exposure. However, the contract had specific provisions for risk allocation between the parties, and quantification flowed directly from the wording of the risk allocation mechanism, irrespective of what either party alleged would be fair or negligent, and the contractual wording took precedence.

As the business was growing, we had another boost in profile when the movie *The Accountant*, starring Ben Affleck, was also released around this time. It's the story of a brilliant forensic accountant, Christian Wolff, who is hired by a tech firm to investigate suspicious financial irregularities, and ultimately uncovers a US$61 million embezzlement and a web of corporate corruption. So far, so realistic.

However, as Wolff digs deeper, people start dying, and he becomes the target of hitmen, as action meets intellect, and forensic accounting meets martial arts. Wolff's back story, autism and illicit work for dangerous criminal organisations, 'un-cooking' the books to expose internal embezzlement, showcase a rare combination of skills – numerical wizardry and highly trained combatant, thanks to his military father.

A lot to unpack, but enough in there for me to spend the next two years introducing myself in presentations as Ben Affleck's better-looking, younger brother, the friendly Forensic Accountant without the criminal associations or violent streak, and more than capable of fighting financial crime (from the office).

Suspicious Minds to Smooth Criminals

It was also good to see that human nature was no different in Australia to what I had experienced in the UK, and Elvis and Michael Jackson would be delighted. There was the usual mix of misappropriation, misconduct and malfeasance, and our investigations covered all sectors from catering to construction, gaming to government agencies and recruitment to retail. There were whistleblower complaints, conflict-of-interest reviews, procurement, integrity and governance reviews, and fraud risk evaluations. It paid to have a suspicious forensic mindset in pursuit of these smooth criminals.

There was also a surge in bribery and corruption cases in the aftermath of the *Panama Papers* scandal of 2016, one of the most significant data leaks in history, from Mossack Fonseca, a Panamanian law firm, which exposed hidden financial dealings, tax evasion, money laundering and sanctions avoidance, involving politicians, celebrities, and business leaders around the globe.

Whilst most of our investigations are confidential and cannot be disclosed, a few made it into public domain, particularly where whistleblowers went public and organisations were reluctantly drawn into the limelight. One long-running investigation and remediation case was for a government agency facing extensive scrutiny from the union and The Fair Work Ombudsman in relation to: under and over payments to staff; incorrect classification of work hours; miscalculation of overtime, leave entitlements and other allowances relative to the requirements of various enterprise bargaining agreements (EBAs).

Our work was to create an intricate model, by individual and by year, setting out a comparison of actual and expected payments for a high volume of individuals, working a range of different shifts over time, with different entitlements and allowances, under a complex series of EBAs over multiple years. A detailed series of calculations was required, involving a mix of objective facts and subjective decisions, which formed the basis of one of the first wage remediation and compliance engagements we had undertaken, with accountabilities to a number of different stakeholders.

As individual calculations, these had to be spot on. Attention to detail, precision, and factual accuracy were paramount in determining the right result at both an organisational and an individual level, ensuring that they could correctly and consistently provide compensation, which would return each individual to the position they should have been in.

The broader context of fraud in Australia was also familiar. Our Fraud Barometer pointed north each year, with almost half of all frauds committed by company management or employees, the most significant growth arising from collusion or professional criminals bringing greater sophistication and technology to targeting organisations, particularly those with weaker defences.

Australia was more exposed than other developed economies at that time, as it had been more than a quarter of a century since its last recession, and a combination of complacency, capability, and lack of investment, meant that some organisations had devoted insufficient resources and know-how to prevention and detection, under-estimating the insider threat, and lacking robust identity and access management controls, meaning they were more exposed when fraudsters and cybercriminals tested their defences.

A further stimulus arrived in the form of the Hayne Royal Commission, which was formally launched at the end of 2017 and came into its own in 2018. It followed intense public scrutiny and media coverage of various instances of alleged misconduct across financial institutions in Australia, with the most lurid headlines being in relation to allegations of deducting fees from dead clients, fees for ongoing advice where no service was provided, improper lending practices, and various financial advice scandals.

One major bank had issues with commission-based incentives for third-party introducers, who referred potential home loan customers. In Western Sydney, bankers had accepted detailed financial documents from unlicensed introducers, and failed to spot allegedly fraudulent payslips, putting the bank at risk of default, and borrowers at risk of receiving loans they could not afford. The Royal Commission referred to *"bribes for loans"* and a high-pressure sales culture, incentivising volumes over suitability, which led to breaches of responsible lending obligations, a detailed remediation programme to compensate customers, as well as regulatory action and reputational damage.

Another major bank was under an enforcement action from the regulator AUSTRAC in relation to: failing to monitor international transactions, including payments linked to child exploitation; allowing unmonitored transfers to the Philippines and Southeast Asia from accounts held by convicted child sex offenders; and breaching anti-money laundering and counter-terrorism financing (AML/CTF) obligations over a multi-year period. This ultimately resulted in a penalty of $1.3 billion, the largest fine in Australian corporate history at that time.

Our 2018 Banking Survey also highlighted the challenges faced by financial institutions, with heightened sector-specific issues including cybercrime, identity theft and account takeover, card-not-present (CNP) fraud, social engineering, investment scams, romance-based scams, cryptocurrency fraud, and tax office and government impersonation. Added to the growing compliance requirements in financial crime, customer due diligence, transactions and sanctions screening, as well as scrutiny and heightened regulatory requirements. It was a tough time for financial institutions.

As we closed on our first full financial year with the new team on board, we had smashed our budget and grown the business by 40%. It was outstanding on every measure, but we were now on the cusp of even more substantial change....

Take On Me

Our A-Ha moment of early 2019 was when we realised that our team of 50, which had quickly grown organically to 75, was now poised to go north of 100 as part of a strategic acquisition by the firm of the boutique restructuring and forensic business, Ferrier Hodgson.

As part of the deal, our Forensic business would add 3 new Partners and 25 staff. As with any integration, it was important to spend the time to understand the strengths, interests and aspirations of both teams, individually and collectively, to articulate the strategic purpose and opportunity from coming together (i.e. areas of complementary capabilities where we were under-strength and they were strong in Disputes and Forensic Technology), and to organise a series of events to introduce the teams on a social level ahead of formally working together.

Many deals fail, and I wasn't willing for that to happen to this one. Significant time and effort was therefore spent on due diligence to fully understand what we were taking on, in defining and articulating the synergies, to integrate the teams, and to ensure there was an appropriate balance, capability and representation for both teams in leadership roles, including service line, sector, office, and practice management responsibilities.

Given the new capabilities, I relinquished all responsibility for Disputes to our new Partners, and for our Melbourne team to another Partner, and I was happy to do so as they were the best people for those roles. It was a delicate balance, but having the right people in the right roles with the right support was vital to set us up for success going forward.

With the rapid increase in scale of the business, integration, opportunity and growth potential, I was also able to invest in a Chief Operating Officer who joined the business one month before the deal went live.

On 1 July 2019, our team was ready for anything… until the world changed again in 2020….

CHAPTER 11

SWIMMING NAKED

"You never know who's swimming naked until the tide goes out."

Warren Buffett, billionaire investor with Berkshire Hathaway, the 'Sage of Omaha'

The Great Pandemic

In late March 2020, we had a Forensic Partner dinner in Sydney, which felt like the last supper. Rumours of hazmat suits and lockdowns swirled all around us, and we joked that this could be our last get-together for months. Little did we know then that the Great Pandemic was just getting going.

The following morning, I flew back to Melbourne, and the first lockdown came into force a few days later. Melbourne was on the verge of becoming the most locked-down city in the world, with 262 cumulative days under stay-at-home orders over the next 19 months.

The fear and uncertainty was tangible everywhere, a surreal mix of concern and compliance with the new rules. At work, we were online overnight, and the transition went remarkably smoothly. From a firm perspective, however, facing a steep downturn in demand across several divisions, decisive measures had to be taken to absorb the financial impact and protect long-term stability.

A combination of hiring and promotion freezes, paid special leave, and temporary pay cuts for staff, plus much larger reductions in Partner incomes, all played their part. We also had to reflect the reality of how deeply and quickly economic conditions had changed, resulting in a small number of redundancies in impacted areas affecting approximately 2% of the workforce overall.

Making people's roles redundant is an unpleasant but occasionally necessary role a leader has to perform. I have now had to do so on seven separate occasions, for fourteen individuals, and the process always deserves as much empathy, compassion, decency and humanity as possible. These meetings were no different, particularly for individuals already facing the distress and worry of what this unknown pandemic would bring.

I hosted a national team call to convey the measures the firm was taking, the underlying rationale, and how it would impact members of our team. The Q&A session at the end, which was scheduled for 20 minutes, ended up taking more than an hour with 75 questions from team members around the country, naturally experiencing the full range of emotional responses. Again, with as much compassion, clarity and honesty as I could muster.

Leadership of people does throw up a number of challenges, and these have been many and varied over the years. We are all human, imperfect, and flawed—I certainly am—and the boundary between work and life will sometimes blur. I've had staff needing support from dealing with harassment to escaping an abusive partner, from alcoholism to financial difficulties, and from mental health to immigration issues, all unconnected with the workplace. I've tried to be supportive and empathetic through all of these. In a similar vein, I've managed through the sudden and traumatic bereavement of colleagues and friends, and the communication and support plan for a staff member transitioning from male to female.

As the team grew, the more people we had, the more people issues we encountered. With more than 100 Partners and staff in our national team, our run rate was typically around one issue, complaint or concern per month. In a high-performing team of smart, competitive people, it was inevitable that not everyone would get along, and a proportion of time was spent on mediation, conciliation and resolving interpersonal issues, the most serious of which, particularly on the few occasions they involved alleged bullying or harassment, had input from our People & Inclusion team.

There have also been the interesting one-off cases over the years: the staff member who announced that he had to leave work to go home as soon as the sun went down for religious reasons (not great during winter, not reciprocated the other way during summer); another who insisted on getting changed for work in the open plan office after running; and one who was allegedly working in a café (actually as a barista *in* the café rather than *from* the café during working hours when also being paid by the firm). I've learned not to be phased by anything but to listen with empathy and a supportive ear, and take each case and individual on merit. As the team grew, I was grateful to have a succession of capable People Partners as the first port of call for these issues, plus support from our COO.

From a work perspective, our portfolio of ongoing cases continued, but there was a worrying drop in new instructions in those first, few months of the pandemic. However, with the benefit of hindsight, this was like that disconcerting, counter-intuitive phenomenon of the tsunami's 'drawback', when sea levels appear to go out dramatically as the trough of the wave first reaches the shore, before the full crest of the tsunami crashes in.

It was in these moments of 'drawback' that Warren Buffett was proved correct, the disruption of the pandemic revealing issues that may otherwise have remained hidden: *"You never know who's swimming naked until the tide goes out."* In the months that followed, from July 2020 onwards, the tsunami of new investigations began to roll in.

The Forensic Lens

COVID-19 had a profound impact on the nature and volume of investigations. There was a surge in historic cases, as fraudulent activity could not be so easily concealed from home, with issues revealed as transaction volumes declined. New cases also emerged as the fraud triangle flashed red: there were *opportunities* in the chaos of the scramble to stabilise businesses; *incentives* through the desperation and anxiety of economic hardship, and actual or expected layoffs; and *rationalisation* as people felt the unfairness of suddenly having to work harder for less, in the face of pay cuts, pay freezes, job insecurity, and lost bonuses, all at a time when other freedoms had been curtailed.

The surge in employee fraud was mirrored by spikes in financial statement fraud, as managers attempted to inflate results to meet bonus targets, particularly tempting in the run-up to 30 June, with hopes otherwise dashed in the final months of the financial year. We were called in to investigate both direct examples of financial mis-statement, and indirect cases of post-year-end irrecoverable debts, customer complaints, and other distress, which ultimately had roots in earlier inflation and manipulation.

As government-sponsored COVID relief schemes were quickly designed and rolled out to support struggling businesses, these were inevitably subject to new forms of fraud, including bogus relief claims and stimulus cheque scams, designed to trick people into disclosing personal or financial information by pretending to offer government-issued economic relief payments. We supported a number of government agencies and insurers with preventative and detective controls, using fraud analytic tools, to improve their chances of finding fraudulent claims, given the speed and volume of applications.

Our forensic lens, experience and expertise were crucial given the rapidly evolving landscape.

Our methodologies also had to evolve as social distancing and travel restrictions precluded on-site investigation and in-person interviewing. This was a real challenge as restricted access to physical records drove reliance on digital documentation, which sometimes slowed the pace of investigation and made it harder to verify authenticity.

Similarly, interviews conducted over Zoom or Teams were naturally more limited in terms of the ability to build trust, rapport and psychological comfort with interviewees, as well as the ability to detect body language, micro-expressions, subtle gestures, and other cues, critical for fraud detection.

The psychological impact of being in the same room—especially in high-stakes or sensitive interviews—can influence behaviour and truthfulness, and interviewees may have felt less compelled to cooperate or disclose information when the investigator was not physically present.

Our dependence on Forensic Technology, Analytics and Cyber Response capabilities also increased, and we invested heavily in these areas. Tech-enabled fraud and cybercrime were growing more rapidly in areas such as credit card fraud, hacking financial systems, fake online ads, electronic transfers and money laundering via betting accounts. Our specialist technology team of around five in 2016 (10% of our national team) had grown to more than 40 by 2022 (30%) and was continuing to grow.

Professional scepticism became even more crucial during remote investigations, as did reliance on insights from whistleblowers and hotline reporting, both of which gained importance as fraud detection tools. As a forerunner of the emerging Gen AI revolution, advanced people skills and technologies were increasingly important in the online world of 2020-22.

In 2021, we conducted a survey, which found that more than half of all Australian businesses included in the survey reported: an increase in fraud risk due to remote working; an increase in cyber-related fraud risk, nearly a quarter saying it rose significantly; more vulnerability to fraud than before the pandemic; a compromise in ability to investigate fraud; uncertainty as to whether all fraud was detected; and employees remained the biggest fraud risk—more than suppliers or contractors.

The survey tallied with our experience that fraud was flashing red as an increasing risk to business, often undetected for years, especially when committed by insiders familiar with company systems. The pandemic had inhibited investigations, and delayed fraud prevention, storing up more problems for the future.

The future for Forensic became the *Forensic Lens* podcast series, launched in 2022, with one of our Partners as the smooth interviewer of a number of esteemed guests in our quest to detect lies, deception and fraud in the world of business.

The Room Where It Happens

Fraud is definitively not a victimless crime, even if it can sometimes appear that way when harm is dispersed or indirect. Businesses suffer loss of revenue, reputational damage, and disruption, often leading to job losses and pay freezes when profitability is eroded. It also increases costs for everyone through higher insurance premiums and taxes, and, when trust in institutions, markets, and governance is undermined, there is a loss of investment and growth for economies as a whole, and shareholders, customers, suppliers, and pension funds, who lose out directly and indirectly from inefficient markets.

Beyond that, at a personal level, individuals can lose their savings, retirement funds, and homes. The emotional and psychological trauma experienced by victims who feel violated, embarrassed, angry, or betrayed—especially in cases of romance scams and insider fraud – cannot be overstated, as stress, anxiety, and depression are common.

Over the years, we have seen striking similarities between fraudsters and corporate psychopaths in the manipulation of systems and people for personal gain. Whilst fraudsters lie to gain money or status, corporate psychopaths lie to gain power or influence.

They are both masters of positive impression management, good communicators, comfortable using language expressively, and carefully craft their personal narrative to build and maintain control in their spheres of interest. They can be charismatic, manipulative, superficially charming, persuasive, and have a high work output, often driven by money, power, and prestige. They will usually befriend and manipulate those with access to informal power or who may be useful to them.

Whilst they mimic emotion, they typically lack true empathy, showing little concern for the harm caused to others, and can abandon people who are no longer useful to them. They are also prone to risk-taking, exploiting loopholes, ignoring ethical boundaries, and are willing to rationalise their actions, seeing manipulation of those around them as a normal part of life.

It is often the most trusted and respected individuals in the organisation who use deceit to encourage others to believe in something untrue, either a lie or a critical omission, in order to create an impression useful to their narrative.

The insight from whistleblowers is therefore invaluable, particularly where there is a marked difference between the impression that junior staff have of an individual, relative to senior management, as the fraudster prioritises managing up the chain of command, and is much less interested and empathetic with junior staff, except where junior staff can be useful or can be manipulated into processing certain transactions or accessing sensitive information.

It is always worth listening to whistleblowers who raise concerns where there is a fundamental mismatch in perceptions, particularly if individuals are identified as arrogant, manipulative, cold-hearted, untrustworthy, or take undue credit for the achievements of others. There may well be something substantive to be uncovered.

The reality of conducting suspect interviews is very different to TV dramas. There is no good-cop-bad-cop routine, aggressive table thumping, or killer questions to make the suspect crumble. The tone is professional, methodical, calm, and carefully constructed to ensure the interview is conducted in accordance with procedural fairness, following protocol in a legally compliant manner.

Building rapport and trust with the interviewee is crucial in terms of tone, content and body language, and the interviewer must be engaging, empathetic, curious, and genuinely interested in understanding the interviewee's perspective and explanation of events. Areas of enquiry are carefully planned and delineated, questions sequenced methodically, evidence introduced appropriately, and everything said is recorded.

The output from interviews is only as good as the questions asked, so it is vital to design and structure questions that have the best chance of extracting the relevant information and evidence.

In the interview room, deception can be difficult to pin down as fraudsters often mix lies and distortions, with elements of truth, even some low-level admissions, in constructing a narrative designed to suit their purpose. Confessions are rare or piecemeal and take time to develop, but outcomes only stand up to scrutiny if the process is properly followed. Admissions are often the tip of an iceberg, a calculation the fraudster makes of what they think they can get away with.

The interview can be a game to them, and when confronted, the story shifts, the narrative changes, and the synthesis becomes a fluid mix of truth and lies, a way of saving face, and landing on the next best alternative. There is often an element of self-deception, an attempt to rationalise and explain, bringing others into the narrative as scapegoats or characters in their story.

The discipline of the interviewer is therefore crucial, as inconsistencies and adjustments in narrative are where the fraudster comes unstuck, as a very good memory is required to maintain consistency of deception with the other salient facts.

In 2020, an explosive new investigation brought together a number of these themes.

A client asked for our assistance, having been made aware of concerns about an employee in its overseas subsidiary, allegedly engaging in bullying and harassment of junior staff, and some unusual activity in the processing of certain transactions. We would normally have mobilised a small, combined team from Australia and overseas to investigate on-site, but this was impossible due to pandemic travel restrictions.

The next best thing was to gather electronic and other evidence in the background, from servers, financial reports, initial interviews, and background forensic intelligence gathering on key individuals. This wasn't as effective as capturing source laptop, phone, and other financial records on-site, but at least provided a baseline insight into the allegations, and was helpful in developing a tailored investigation plan.

It soon became clear that we had opened a can of worms, and the consequences wriggled in all directions. The documents and emails raised further concerns, as the intelligence gathering demonstrated some unusual links between individuals and companies, including potential conflicts of interest. Once one interviewee turned whistleblower, creating a safe environment for concerns to be raised, others began to come forward.

More serious allegations emerged, as initial concerns were soon swamped by a series of systemic issues, including allegations of: fictitious accounting entries; suspicious payments; related party transactions where funds appeared to be misappropriated to companies ultimately owned by a senior official in the subsidiary; payments to third parties, which acted as an intermediary to another company, effectively used to pay kickbacks to senior officials in the subsidiary; payments and gifts to government officials and other consultants, which may have been illegal bribes to win contracts; and procurement and contracting issues, secret commissions, and other breaches of fraud and corruption policies.

These were explosive allegations, and in the detailed interviews which followed online via Teams, more interviewees became whistleblowers, confessions were obtained in some key areas (notably, in relation to a backpack of cash used to pay bonuses), and we painstakingly built a picture of the key individuals in the subsidiary, systematically appearing to use their positions to extract value from the parent company for personal gain.

Whilst some interviews were successful, the process via Teams was frustrating, as it was naturally more difficult to build rapport and connection, and more tempting for certain interviewees to obfuscate and deflect, often blaming deficiencies in technology when wanting to avoid certain questions, than would have been the case if we had been on-site in the room.

Nonetheless, our structured questioning paved the way for meaningful outputs, and the evidence obtained across the investigation was compelling. We had effectively proved that investigations could adapt quickly to a high-tech online world, but the optimum conditions for interviews were always going to take place in the room where it happens.

The World Turns Again

In 2022, Australia was ranked 13th of 180 countries in Transparency International's Corruption Perception Index, the league table of perceived levels of public sector corruption. Having dropped out of the top 10, there was renewed focus on improving Australia's response to foreign bribery and corruption, which, similar to fraud, is not a victimless crime.

As one company gains an advantage by paying government officials to win contracts (unless they are caught), others lose out, markets become distorted and inefficient, companies rely on shortcuts rather than quality and innovation, erosion of trust weakens confidence in institutions, and rising inequality benefits the powerful at the expense of the weak.

During the pandemic, an increasing number of companies identified issues of potential bribery overseas, either directly or via whistleblowers, and began to take more responsibility for disclosure of incidents, as well as prevention, detection and risk management. We helped a number of organisations through the process of investigation and self-disclosure to the authorities (always much better than responding to a regulatory notice), sometimes in response to whistleblower incidents in the press, and others that emerged internally.

One incident arose as a demand for payment for a personal property extension by a government official, and another was identified as a request by an agent to manipulate financial records. We also did some meaningful work to help raise defences by designing effective risk assessments, policies and procedures, integrity due diligence reviews on employees, agents, contractors, and business partners, as well as developing communication and training programmes, and monitoring, reporting and whistleblowing regimes.

A crucial component is always getting the 'tone at the top' right, with senior leaders actively promoting zero-tolerance towards fraud, bribery and corruption, and visibly supporting anti-bribery initiatives. Senior executives have the single biggest influence on corporate culture and, when working effectively, this cascades throughout the organisation.

Peer pressure towards integrity and values-based culture is important where individuals are held to account, not only in what is said in boardrooms, but also what is unsaid, the bottom line on acceptable behaviour, and the mindset applied when dealing with ethical dilemmas – for example, when assessing potential conflicts of interest, having to chooses between profitability and environmental responsibility, and human rights or supply chains.

A close cousin of corruption is modern slavery. In 2022, an estimated 50 million people in the world were living as victims of modern slavery. At work, this includes everything from forced labour, where people are coerced to work under threat of consequences, to debt bondage, where work is demanded to repay loans under unfair terms. It also includes forced marriage, where individuals are compelled to marry without consent, human trafficking, sexual exploitation, via coerced or deceptive involvement in sex work, and domestic servitude.

A staggering 71% of all people trapped in modern slavery worldwide are women and girls. The same characteristics of deception, lies and concealment are often present when vulnerable people are drawn into modern slavery, particularly in industries such as agriculture, construction, domestic work, cleaning, hospitality, meat processing and food services.

The Australian Modern Slavery Act came into effect on 1 January 2019, with a view to addressing modern slavery in business operations and supply chains, and included mandatory reporting requirements for businesses of a certain size. Whilst few companies knowingly support modern slavery practices, a number of our investigations over the years have touched on instances, that directly or indirectly indicated potential breaches.

For example, in one case where security was outsourced to a third-party provider, a number of foreign students who appeared to be working up to the allowable threshold number of hours per week, were actually working much longer hours, at below minimum wage rates, and had their passports withheld as part of the working arrangement, in what was effectively a case of wage theft and coercion.

In another case, a whistleblower raised allegations of exploitative work practices at an overseas operation, which included forced labour, excessive working hours, unpaid overtime, no worker rights, and poor and hazardous working conditions. Interestingly, a previous review had not identified any issues, as the practices had been concealed during an on-site visit. Companies must therefore be vigilant and aware of how insidious and hidden these practices can be, as modern slavery often has metaphorical rather than literal chains.

At a corporate level, there are risks of cartel and stock market manipulation, which sometimes lead to investigations. Cartel behaviour is illegal, anti-competitive cooperation between competing businesses to limit competition, and manipulate the market in areas such as price fixing, bid-rigging coordination as to who will win tenders and at what price, dividing customers to avoid competition and limiting the supply of goods or services to drive up prices.

Cartels effectively act against the interests of consumers, often resulting in higher prices, reduced choice, poorer service delivery, and inefficient markets. The cases we have been involved in have required investigation of both the evidence of cartel behaviour, in terms of correspondence, contracts, communications and indications of collaboration, and the consequential impact, in terms of economic outcomes, pricing decisions, bid patterns, and market allocations.

Similar to cases of bribery and corruption, once the Board becomes aware of potential cartel activity in one of its divisions, it must cease the conduct immediately, and consider both an independent investigation and voluntary disclosure to the ACCC, the regulator responsible for fair and competitive markets in Australia, which may include an application for immunity, as well as reviewing its compliance procedures to prevent any future breaches.

It is a similar story with stock market manipulation cases, such as insider trading, failure to disclose material information to the market, breaches of corporate disclosure rules, and intentionally spreading false or misleading information. These can have serious consequences, leading to company failures, loss of jobs, and shareholder class action lawsuits, which often follow. The vast majority of people have exposure to the financial markets, whether through savings, investments, or retirement funds. When markets are skewed or inefficient, everyone loses.

Perhaps the single biggest change over the past few years has been the rise of cybercrime, which has surged dramatically over the past decade, with Australia losing billions of dollars annually. A recent Cyber Threat Report highlighted a continued deterioration in Australia's cybersecurity environment, with the government now committing $15–20 billion to develop more robust cyber defence capabilities. Cybercrime is causing havoc, drawing nations into war, and companies into economic difficulties, as criminal gangs and state-sponsored threat actors co-ordinate cross-border attacks across the dark web.

Over the past few years, Ransomware attacks have become much more frequent and sophisticated, with the rise of Ransomware-as-a-Service (RaaS), platforms allowing even low-skilled threat actors to launch attacks, with targets including hospitals, governments, and critical infrastructure. With Advanced Persistent Threats (APTs), cybercriminals have also shifted from simple malware attacks to stealthier, longer-term intrusions, infiltrating systems quietly, often for espionage or data theft.

Similarly, digital payment and cryptocurrencies have also enabled anonymous money laundering and ransom payments, with online fraud, phishing attacks, deepfakes, and other scams, constantly adapting to exploit digital wallets and mobile banking.

The most significant denial of service attacks can shut down or compromise key systems, steal sensitive customer and financial data, as well as trade secrets, and the true extent of the data loss or compromise may never be known. The impact of a cyber-attack can be extensive, not only in terms of out-of-pocket costs, including whether or not to pay the ransom, but also disruption to the business, remediation and security uplift, legal costs and regulatory actions.

However, the largest loss often comes from the reputational damage over time as customers and the markets lose confidence in continuing with the business. Over the past few years, we significantly increased our investment in cybersecurity, incident response and intelligence capabilities, supporting numerous clients to help prevent, detect and ultimately respond to cyber incidents across their operations. This is only going to continue.

The next big change on the horizon was emergence of agentic AI, which can act with autonomy and contextual decision-making to enhance investigations. As early as 2022, AI was beginning to transform the world of forensic accounting, improving speed, accuracy, and refinement in the scoping of investigations. Accelerated forensic analytics, advanced fraud detection models, and the automation of routine tasks, which would previously have been the domain of investigation teams, were beginning to be deployed in more meaningful ways. The right data analytic algorithms can more quickly identify potentially suspicious transactions, inconsistencies and anomalies, and unusual patterns or red flag indicators of fraud or financial misconduct. Natural language processing also allows AI to analyse unstructured data such as emails, contracts, and reports, to uncover potential hidden relationships or deceptive language, thereby expanding the scope of investigations, with repetitive tasks such as data entry, reconciliations, and email review being increasingly automated. In addition, machine learning models are now increasingly capable of being trained to detect potential subtle indicators of fraud based on the ingestion and review of the wealth of historical cases.

As with any advance in technology, the role of forensic accountants will not be replaced but will be refined to focus on leveraging AI insights, interpreting results (including removal of false positives), conducting higher-level analysis, and strategic decision-making. Whilst AI boosts efficiency, it also introduces risks, for which the traditional forensic toolkit – a curious and sceptical mindset, and quality of thinking, challenge and questioning – will be vital to address the potential for over-reliance on algorithms, bias in AI models, and data privacy concerns. In this context, human oversight by forensic experts will remain essential in the deployment of AI in investigations in a way that maintains trust, transparency and integrity, and ethical and accurate outcomes.

Speed Swimmers

By the end of 2022, the worst of the pandemic was over, and our Forensic team had swum faster and stronger than ever before. We had trebled the business in 5 years, growing the team to more than 150 Partners and staff in that time. We hadn't been caught swimming naked but had instead swum through the crest of the wave, focusing in the right areas, with the right people, doing the right things to be successful.

As I thought about the future, I referred again to the 'Sage of Omaha', reflecting on his advice that: *"The best investment you can make, is an investment in yourself, the more you learn, the more you'll earn…..The difference between successful people and really successful people is that really successful people say no to almost everything…. There comes a time when you ought to start doing what you want. Take a job that you love. You will jump out of bed in the morning. I think you are out of your mind if you keep taking jobs that you don't like because you think it will look good on your resume. Isn't that a little like saving up sex for your old age?"*

I had turned 50 in 2022, and it was time to invest in myself, say no to a few things and have a little fun…

**International man of mystery at the International
Bar Association Conference in Tokyo, 2014**

Have kilt, will travel – my Scottish roots and heritage is never far from the surface - at a formal event in Melbourne, 2023

CHAPTER 12

WINNING AND INFLUENCING

"Happiness doesn't depend upon who you are or what you have; it depends solely upon what you think. So, start each day by thinking of all the things you have to be thankful for. Your future will depend very largely on the thoughts you think today. So, think thoughts of hope and confidence and love and success."

Dale Carnegie, from the book
How to Win Friends and Influence People

Faster, Higher, Stronger

As a teenage boy, I was inspired by Billy Connolly to become windswept and interesting.

Over the Christmas holidays at the end of 2022, I reflected on who I wanted to become now I had entered my 50s and, as Billy says, *"I've spent a great deal of my life being a boy, being excited by things, and it has done me good... I've never recovered from that, and I have no intention of doing so."*

Over the following 6 months, as my thinking developed, a series of revelations gradually became clearer, which made me excited about the possibilities for my next chapter.

I reflected on the start of my career in Forensic in London, the work I was doing, and the importance of my values – seeking positive Meaning, Authenticity, Reflection, Team-impact, Integrity, and what was Natural to me.

I thought about going *Faster*, inspired by the Olympic ideals and the challenges faced and overcome by Cathy Freeman in the 2000 Sydney Olympics.

I thought about going *Higher*, and the courage, curiosity and perseverance, shown by Marie Curie in becoming the first female Nobel Prize winner and changing the world in the process.

I also thought about getting *Stronger*, and it was here that my first revelation came.

During the course of 2022, our leadership team completed the Gallup Clifton StrengthsFinder, a development tool designed to help individuals and groups identify and harness their natural talents or strengths. It flips the script of the traditional model of personal development, which focuses on fixing weaknesses, and concentrates on helping individuals become aware of, and build on, their strengths.

The model works by way of questionnaire to develop a personalised, ordered list of 34 strengths, covering the four key domains of:

- Execution (a task orientation to get things done);
- Influencing (a people orientation to lead and persuade);
- Relationship Building (a team orientation of strong personal relationships); and

- Strategic Thinking (an ideas orientation around strategic direction).

For those of you who know me well, it will come as no surprise that none of my top 10 strengths were in Execution, although my representation across each of the other domains meant that I could think strategically, across my relationships, to influence others in the team to execute tasks as required. For the record, my top ten strengths included:

- Woo, Maximiser, Communication, and Activator (Influencing);
- Positivity, Connectedness, Adaptability, and Empathy (Relationship Building); and
- Context and Strategic (Strategic Thinking).

The focus on strengths was helpful in 3 ways.

Firstly, it shone a light on the strengths of our current and emerging leadership team, and clarified who would be most suited, motivated and capable of taking on different roles.

Secondly, it clarified for me where my strengths were, as well as how others may perceive the negatives of those strengths. For example, the hilariously entitled Woo was my #3 strength overall, which was great for energising, networking and connecting with people, but for those where Woo was lower-ranked, the risk was that my strength could potentially come across as shallow or insincere.

And finally, awareness of my strengths was helpful in planning the types of roles I should pursue (those making the most of my high-end strengths) and roles I should avoid (those requiring me to use my lower-ranked strengths), irrespective of how impressive or useful these may be perceived to be from a career perspective. It reminded me of a Corporates role I did for a couple of years with a view to career development, which I did well enough, but it tied me up in internal meetings and tasks, which I didn't enjoy, when there was a high opportunity cost to what else I could have been doing.

As the pandemic's pause gave way to a faster pace, and expectations rose once again, I made a decision not to push faster and higher from a career perspective, but to invest in myself, build my strengths, and apply those strengths in roles I would enjoy.

Win-Win

Winning can mean different things to different people, and can include a wide range of outcomes and mindsets.

From a sporting perspective, my heroes were Sir Alex Ferguson and Tom Brady, unrivalled in winning more titles than anyone else in their chosen fields. And whilst their legacies had deeper lessons around leadership, culture, communication, and continuous learning, their winning mindset was key, as Brady said: *"The true competitors are the ones who always play to win."*

However, playing to win also exposed them to the risk of losing, and the need to build resilience when losing battles, but remaining focused on winning titles, was beautifully illustrated by another celebrated sporting icon, tennis legend Roger Federer, winner of an unprecedented (at the time) 20 Grand Slam men's singles titles.

In 2024, after retirement, Federer spoke about the importance of not dwelling on disappointments, and what he called the *'4% rule'*, where small margins, and an ability to manage your mindset, make all the difference between good and great. Federer said, *"I won only 54% of the points I played. Which means I lost 46%. And yet I won 80% of my matches."*

From a business perspective, I had experienced strategic wins through targeted recruitment in new areas, solving complex problems, winning cases, and helping the practice grow. I also had my fair share of reverses, losing client tenders, cases that didn't go as well as expected, key people leaving, and other disappointments along the way.

Over time, I learned to treat those failures as an important part of the journey, as opportunities to learn, and to let those failures refine me, rather than define me. Dale Carnegie had a similar approach when he said, *"Develop success from failures. Discouragement and failure are two of the surest stepping stones to success."*

In Carnegie's famous tome, *How to Win Friends and Influence People*, he talks about the importance of being able to understand the perspective of the other person, and seek areas of mutual benefit and collaboration as key to achieving win-win outcomes for everyone. His principles are simple and easy to adopt: be likeable, empathetic, and genuinely interested in other people; always talk about the other person's interests, desires and ideas; always praise, encourage and appreciate sincerely; and never criticise or argue.

There are numerous examples of how these attributes benefit both the person exhibiting them, and the other person, in finding areas of mutual benefit, literally helping to build positive relationships, win friends and influence other people. No matter what business or role you are in, the mindset of taking time to understand the people at the centre of what you are trying to achieve is always worth the investment.

In 2022-2023, I had access to a personal coach for the first time in my career. By this point, I had been doing the same role for almost 6 years, and whilst I enjoyed most aspects of it, I did appreciate the opportunity to have space and time for some facilitated thinking around what would come next, where I wanted to go, and what I wanted to do.

As a result of those coaching sessions, I had my second revelation.

Coaching consolidated my thinking that whilst I wasn't pushing higher, I was deeply embedded in the world of Forensic, and discovered that I was interested in deploying my experience to have a broader impact on the global Forensic practice.

Whilst challenging to do from Australia, given the distance from the rest of the world and inhospitable time zones, which meant calls would take place late in the evening, I was motivated to find out more. I was also well placed to add value. I was one of the longer-standing national Forensic practice leaders in the global firm, and with the development of the practice, Australia had grown from the 13th to the 5th largest practice in the firm in that time.

I expressed my interest to the relevant global leaders and, when opportunity next arose, I was appointed to take on a new role as Global Head of Forensic Networks & Solutions, with responsibility on the Global Forensic Steering Group for supporting, leading and mentoring our global leaders for each of our major service lines – Disputes, Investigations, Ethics & Compliance, Forensic Technology, Financial Crime and Third Party Risk Management – helping them invest, grow, and develop the impact of their services, and connect, collaborate and contribute to helping them work with leaders across our global network, which had withered to some extent as a result of the pandemic.

My experience of running a national practice in Australia, with teams delivering across the majority of service lines, combined with my connections within the firm, including my time in the UK, gave me confidence that I could add meaningful value here and be excited about the possibilities of doing so. I was also able to balance the challenge of periodic late-night calls with the benefits of accessing the best insights from around the world, providing strategic thinking, and influence on opportunities, including for our Australian team, and improving connectivity with global leaders on calls and in-person events in Japan, Germany, and the USA over the following 18 months.

I also found the coaching experience fascinating in other ways. The facilitated nature of the coaching conversation, and the nature and structuring of the questions, gave me a forum in which I could think more deeply and meaningfully about what I really wanted than I would normally have done. I felt more self-aware of my strengths and capabilities, my leadership style and impact, and how I could bring more of my strategic thinking and influencing skills to bear in my role.

I was also more aware of the impact that emotional intelligence and empathy could have on some of my interactions, as I became better at building trust and collaboration across teams as a result of these reflections. I had a curiosity and interest in questions and listening through my forensic work, as well as my strengths, so it was a natural extension of this to be able to explore things through the crucible of the coaching relationship.

It was here that my third revelation came.

I decided that I wanted to follow in the footsteps of Sir Alex Ferguson and develop my own skills as a coach. I have been very fortunate in my career to have been able to work in some high-performing environments and with some exceptional people. I have also spent the last couple of decades in a variety of leadership roles, having a modicum of success and gaining a wealth of experience.

On turning 50, I felt it was time to invest in myself, to become better equipped to be able to give back and support the next generation of leaders coming through, both inside the firm and in business more generally.

I therefore embarked on a series of courses with The Institute of Executive Coaching and Leadership (IECL), obtaining my qualifications to become a Certified and Accredited Executive Coach covering the fundamentals of high-performance organisational coaching, contracting, systems thinking, relational intelligence, perspective-shifting, and applied coaching conversations.

I thoroughly enjoyed being back in the classroom, investing in my skills, and learning a structured approach to coaching, with a view to being able to acquire a new skillset that would create an environment to help others succeed. I felt that the fusion of my leadership experience, combined with a formal coaching skillset, would potentially be interesting to others who may wish to benefit from a coach.

Over the past 12 months, I spent a proportion of my time developing my coaching skills and portfolio, working with a small cohort of people, and bringing my perspective as a Forensic Coach, to help individuals across a number of different sectors and industries to engage in a facilitated coaching process of self-reflection and discovery, as they think about aspects of their career and future direction.

All with a view to helping people unlock their potential and fulfil their dreams.

Follow the Money, Fulfil Your Dreams

I've been fortunate to have had a great experience as a Forensic Consultant in the world of heroes and villains—I've found the smoking guns, I've known where the bodies were buried, and I've caught the bad guys.

So, what have I learned from all those bad guys like Capone, Madoff and Abagnale, and the good guys like Wilson, Markopolos, and Buffett, all of whom followed the money in their own unique ways?

The villains all had similar core characteristics, using deception and exploitation of trust to perpetrate their crimes: Capone using bribery, intimidation, his political connections and his Robin Hood style persona; Madoff trading off his respectable reputation to create a sophisticated parallel front, and fictitious paper trail, to hoodwink investors; and Abagnale using confidence, creativity and craftsmanship in his fabrication of identities and forged cheques.

However, all of their schemes required increasingly desperate and more elaborate concealment before ultimately crashing down.

As Michael Corleone found in The Godfather Part III: *"Just when I thought I was out, they pull me back in."* In the long run, crime doesn't pay, and there is rarely an escape for empires built on fraud, any short-term gains are almost always outweighed to some extent by paranoia, guilt, stress and remorse, and ultimately the loss of freedom, reputation, financial ruin and legal consequences. Capone went from riches to ruin and was imprisoned in Alcatraz, Madoff was sentenced to 150 years imprisonment and died alone, estranged from his family, and Abagnale, exhausted from being on the run, lost it all and was sent to prison.

On the other hand, for heroes such as Wilson and Markopolos, the relentless pursuit of truth, with curiosity and courage, dogged determination and analytical mastery, paved the way, in the long run, to the real reward of bringing down the bad guys. Doing the right things consistently left a legacy of integrity, re-shaping how financial crimes are investigated, how the law can be used for good, and how reform in financial regulation and whistleblower protection can benefit society as a whole. Two men, born decades apart, armed with calculation and conviction, proved that sometimes the most powerful weapon against corruption is a spreadsheet and a stubborn sense of justice.

For Buffet, integrity, honesty and transparency has been a fundamental cornerstone of his entire philosophy and a strategic filter for the partnerships and investments he is willing to make, proving you can be successful in business in an ethical manner and that long-term success isn't just about numbers —it's about trust, reputation, and doing the right thing when no one is watching.

I love the quotes where he says, *"In looking for people to hire, you look for three qualities: integrity, intelligence, and energy. And if you don't have the first, the other two will kill you. You think about it; it's true. If you hire somebody without [integrity], you really want them to be dumb and lazy."*

Similarly, *"Lose money for the firm, and I will be understanding. Lose a shred of reputation for the firm, and I will be ruthless,"* because *"It takes 20 years to build a reputation and five minutes to ruin it. If you think about that, you'll do things differently."*

The science says that money does not bring happiness beyond a certain income threshold.

We adapt quickly to each new level of wealth or income, and the thrill of the raise, or new car, or new house subsides quickly back to our baseline. Our risk is being trapped on the hedonic treadmill, pursuing extrinsic money-driven goals of status and possessions without ever being truly satisfied. More money can mean more pressure, stress and isolation, with longer hours, higher expectations, and less time for relationships, and wealth can also create social distance, making it harder to form genuine connections. Money can certainly play a part in relieving financial stress, and buying comfort, security, and moments of joy, but it's not the ticket to lasting happiness, with satisfaction more deeply connected to intrinsic values like purpose, relationships, meaningful connections, shared experiences and fulfilment.

Andrew Carnegie, one of the wealthiest men of his time, certainly knew this, saying: *"I spent the first half of my life making money and the second half of my life giving it away to do the most good, and the least harm."* His legacy is not just in the buildings that bear his name, but in the values of generosity, responsibility, and moral clarity that he championed and the integrity of his approach. Following the money is important up to a point, but fulfilling your dreams with integrity and character is even more so.

Professional health, wealth and happiness

Dale Carnegie has a fantastic quote on the right lens through which to view success and happiness when he says, *"Success is getting what you want. Happiness is wanting what you get."*

Success and winning is contextual to every individual: the goals we set, the sacrifices we make; the follow-through and drive we have to achieve our goals; and the setbacks and failures along the way, which may or may not be within our control. Happiness, or contentment, on the other hand, is largely derived from the mindset we choose to adopt in *response* to circumstances or outcomes, deserved or otherwise. Unlike success, which often has external factors outside our control, happiness is, to at least some degree, intrinsic, within our grasp, and the mindset we choose to adopt.

This certainly isn't always easy as life challenges us every day, but the path to professional health, wealth and happiness, with all its twists and turns, becomes easier to navigate with the route map of our mindset, and the habits we adopt to build emotional resilience, gratitude and purpose into our lives.

For me, true professional health, wealth and happiness is holistic, balancing work and personal well-being, financial security and fulfilment. It's not just about climbing the corporate ladder or earning more — it's about thriving in all dimensions of life – and the right mindset is the key.

From a work perspective, it's about being in a place where you feel engaged and valued, have a meaningful purpose, aligned to your personal values, as well as work-life balance, positive relationships with your colleagues, and managing energy to avoid burnout.

From a financial perspective, it goes beyond money, which, if over-represented as a driver, can lead to the wrong roles, in the wrong places, at the wrong times. It is more about financial security, freedom, and resourcefulness, an approach to smart planning, saving, investing, and living within your means, but also having the time and energy to enjoy what you have.

In terms of happiness, contentment, positive relationships, purpose, gratitude, and personal growth, these often come as a result of harmony between your professional life and personal values.

Over time, I've come to see the importance of trying to balance the different aspects of my life, to maintain a mindset that aligns with my skills and strengths, as well as my values of doing Meaningful work, being Authentic to who I am, Reflective on what I'm experiencing, conscious of the impact on my Team, aligned with my Integrity, and Natural to me.

My approach has been to try to blend the skills acquired in *what* I do, with the strengths I have and the mindset I apply to *how* I do it, and how I interpret the world around me. A forensic mindset for me is therefore a blend of the skills and strengths I have to seek the truth, establish the facts, look at objective evidence, with attention to detail, understanding the sometimes complex and contradictory motivations of human nature, and having a sceptical radar when people are trying to sell me a story.

I've also developed skills and strengths in asking questions, being genuinely curious and interested in people, listening attentively, and thinking deeply. I've found those to be helpful in both what I do and how I've been able to build a modicum of professional health, wealth and happiness. However, these are not skills that are exclusive in any way, and there are no barriers to entry for anyone developing a similar forensic mindset. As with everything, it just takes time, practice and application to do so.

Some of those skills may not be relevant for you, but there is no harm in asking yourself what skills you've honed from what you do, what strengths you have naturally, how you might deploy them in your roles, and how you develop your own mindset in interpreting the world around you.

In this context, I love the quote from Buffet where he says: *"The people who are most successful are those who are doing what they love…. you only get one mind and one body. And it's got to last a lifetime…. It's what you do right now, today, that determines how your mind and body will operate ten, twenty, and thirty years from now."*

Precious Years

At the beginning of 2025, I made a New Year's resolution to write this book, and in the middle of the year, I took a couple of months of sabbatical leave to do so. It has been a voyage of self-discovery, reminiscence, and revelation, and I have thoroughly enjoyed the journey.

I may be a little nearer the end of my career than the beginning but there are many and varied adventures to come, and I'm reminded of one of my favourite songs, "Precious Years," by the Scottish band, Runrig, which has some poignant words of reflection in the chorus, which we played at Sally's Mum's funeral a few years ago. I definitely recommend having a listen to the gentle melody, poignant lyrics and Donnie Munro's dulcet tones.

These are precious years—I've been grateful to have them, and for those that still are to come. I have loved being a Forensic Consultant, and all the opportunities, experiences, people and places, heroes and villains, I have encountered along the way, and those I am yet to meet in future.

Shining a light on any role can make it sound interesting or dull, and whilst I've tried to pick out the James Bond moments in this book, I hope you have enjoyed this trip down memory lane with me, and that you, too, make the most of the precious years ahead to fulfil your dreams.

May health, wealth and happiness come your way too.

AFTERWORD

This book may close, but the work of the Forensic Consultant goes on - quietly, rigorously, relentlessly, and often unseen. We are not the headline-makers, but the headline-explainers, not the architects of failure, but cartographers, mapping the sources, origins, and evidence of truth in a world of deception.

In these pages, I've tried to capture the tools, techniques and technologies of forensic consulting, and the stories, cases and characters involved. The forensic mindset is key: sceptical, curious, constructive, disciplined, relentless and reflective. It's a profession that demands both precision and empathy— behind every ledger entry is a human decision and a story worth understanding.

As you walk this path, follow your instincts and engage your senses: ask that question, listen intently, notice the silence, see what others overlook. The truth rarely shouts—it waits to be found.

Thank you for joining me on this journey to be windswept and interesting, curious and courageous…. the next case awaits….

— Martin Dougall

ABOUT THE AUTHOR

Martin Dougall is Global Head of Forensic Networks & Solutions at a Big 4 professional services firm. He has spent over thirty years following the money and fulfilling his dreams, from Scotland to Sydney, and Manchester to Melbourne. A forensic accountant by training and detective by instinct, his exposure of fraud and financial crime has shaken industries around the world. From boardroom blunders to billion-dollar breaches and courtroom dramas as an experienced expert witness, Martin has seen it all. But his greatest discovery isn't just where the financial bodies are buried, it's the mindset behind the mission—a forensic way of thinking, blending curiosity, courage, and clarity, with a dash of wit, wisdom and sparkle. In *The Forensic Consultant*, he shares that mindset with readers, offering a blueprint for unlocking professional health, wealth, and happiness. No matter your field, these insights will sharpen your instincts and elevate your impact.

Martin is also a Chartered Accountant, an IECL Accredited Executive Coach, an advisor to Boards, and a professional speaker. This debut book, *The Forensic Consultant*, is part memoir and part guide to anyone looking to build a professional career. Having worked all over the world, Martin is now happily settled in Melbourne, and energised by the opportunity to help people find the clarity of mindset and understanding of strengths to fulfil their dreams. If you would like to know more, please contact the author at: martin.dougall@hotmail.co.uk.

APPENDIX

As promised, here is a diverse set of guiding principles, attributes and values you may want to select from as you define your own personal suite of traits, principles, qualities and ideals:

Acceptance, Accessibility, Accountability, Accuracy, Achievement, Adaptability, Adventure, Affection, Agility, Alertness, Altruism, Ambition, Amusement, Appreciation, Assertiveness, Attentiveness, Authenticity, Awareness, Balance, Beauty, Belonging, Benevolence, Boldness, Bravery, Brilliance, Calmness, Candor, Care, Caring, Caution, Challenge, Charity, Chastity, Cheerfulness, Clarity, Cleanliness, Collaboration, Commitment, Communication, Community, Compassion, Competence, Confidence, Conformity, Connection, Consciousness, Consistency, Contentment, Continuity, Contribution, Control, Conviction, Cooperation, Courage, Courtesy, Creativity, Curiosity, Decisiveness, Dedication, Delight, Dependability, Determination, Development, Devotion, Dignity, Diligence, Diplomacy, Direction, Discipline, Discovery, Diversity, Drive, Duty, Eagerness, Education, Effectiveness, Efficiency, Elegance, Empathy, Empowerment, Encouragement, Endurance, Energy, Enjoyment, Enlightenment, Enthusiasm, Equality, Equanimity, Ethics, Excellence, Excitement, Experience, Expertise, Exploration, Expressiveness, Fairness, Faith, Fame, Family, Fascination, Fidelity, Flexibility, Flow, Focus, Forgiveness, Fortitude, Freedom, Friendship, Frugality, Fun, Generosity, Genius,

Gentleness, Giving, Goodness, Grace, Gratitude, Growth, Guidance, Happiness, Harmony, Health, Helpfulness, Heroism, Holiness, Honesty, Honor, Hope, Hospitality, Humility, Humour, Hygiene, Imagination, Impact, Independence, Individuality, Influence, Ingenuity, Initiative, Innovation, Insight, Inspiration, Integrity, Intelligence, Intensity, Intimacy, Intuition, Inventiveness, Joy, Justice, Kindness, Knowledge, Leadership, Learning, Liberty, Logic, Love, Loyalty, Mastery, Maturity, Meaning, Moderation, Motivation, Natural, Neatness, Nobility, Nonviolence, Nurturing, Obedience, Objectivity, Open-mindedness, Openness, Optimism, Order, Organization, Originality, Ownership, Passion, Patience, Peace, Perceptiveness, Perfection, Perseverance, Persistence, Personal growth, Philanthropy, Playfulness, Pleasure, Poise, Potential, Power, Precision, Preparedness, Presence, Pride, Privacy, Proactivity, Productivity, Professionalism, Progress, Prosperity, Protection, Prudence, Punctuality, Purpose, Quality, Quietness, Rationality, Recognition, Recreation, Reflection, Reliability, Resilience, Resourcefulness, Respect, Responsibility, Rest, Reverence, Rigor, Sacrifice, Safety, Satisfaction, Security, Self-awareness, Self-control, Self-discipline, Self-expression, Selflessness, Sensitivity, Serenity, Service, Sharing, Silence, Simplicity, Sincerity, Skill, Solidarity, Spirituality, Spontaneity, Stability, Stewardship, Strength, Structure, Success, Support, Surprise, Sustainability, Sympathy, Synergy, Systematic, Team-Impact, Teamwork, Temperance, Thankfulness, Thoroughness, Thoughtfulness, Tolerance, Tradition, Tranquillity, Transparency, Trust, Trustworthiness, Truth, Understanding, Uniqueness, Unity, Usefulness, Valor, Variety, Victory, Vigilance, Virtue, Vision, Vitality, Warmth, Wealth, Willpower, Wisdom, Wonder, Young-at-Heart, Zeal

NOTES